Age Smart

Discovering the Fountain of Youth at Midlife and Beyond

Jeffrey Rosensweig, Ph.D.

Betty Liu

PEARSON
Prentice Hall

Upper Saddle River • New York • London • San Francisco • Toronto • Sydney
Tokyo • Singapore • Hong Kong • Cape Town • Madrid
Paris • Milan • Munich • Amsterdam

Vice President and Editor-in-Chief: Tim Moore
Executive Editor: Jim Boyd
Editorial Assistant: Susie Abraham
Development Editor: Russ Hall
Associate Editor-in-Chief and Director of Marketing: Amy Neidlinger
Cover Designer: Solid State Graphics
Managing Editor: Gina Kanouse
Project Editor: Kayla Dugger
Copy Editor: Deadline Driven Publishing
Senior Indexer: Cheryl Lenser
Proofreader: San Dee Phillips
Senior Compositor: Gloria Schurick
Manufacturing Buyer: Dan Uhrig

© 2006 by Jeffrey Rosensweig and Betty Liu
Publishing as Prentice Hall
Upper Saddle River, New Jersey 07458

Prentice Hall offers excellent discounts on this book when ordered in quantity for bulk purchases or special sales. For more information, please contact U.S. Corporate and Government Sales, 1-800-382-3419, corpsales@pearsontechgroup.com. For sales outside the U.S., please contact International Sales, 1-317-581-3793, international@pearsontech-group.com.

Company and product names mentioned herein are the trademarks or registered trademarks of their respective owners.

Printed in the United States of America

Third Printing January, 2008

ISBN-10: 0-13-273678-0

ISBN-13: 978- 0-13-273678-7

Library of Congress Cataloging-in-Publication Data is on file.

This product is printed digitally on demand. This book is the paperback version of an original hardcover book.

Pearson Education LTD.
Pearson Education Australia PTY, Limited.
Pearson Education Singapore, Pte. Ltd.
Pearson Education North Asia, Ltd.
Pearson Education Canada, Ltd.
Pearson Educatión de Mexico, S.A. de C.V.
Pearson Education—Japan
Pearson Education Malaysia, Pte. Ltd.

To Rita, Maria, and John: my inspirations for happy and active longevity.
—J

To Bill, Dad, Anne, and the two biggest reasons why I want to age smart—Dylan and Zachary.
—B

CONTENTS

Acknowledgments

First and foremost, this book would not have happened without the support of the authors' families. Jeff would like to thank his wife, Rita, and his children, Maria and John, while Betty would like to thank her extended family, including her sister, Anne, and her father, who helped her juggle hectic baby schedules while writing this book. As we discuss in *Age Smart*, supportive partners and family members are key to success and longevity.

We'd also like to thank the always intelligent and skilled work of Lori Sullivan, an honors Biology and M.B.A. graduate who works with Jeff as an instructor at Emory University. Lori was the respected "third brain" contributing to this book. Her invaluable research and insight helped improve this book in many ways. We are grateful to the incomparably talented Randi Strumlauf, who charged through hours of interview tapes in short notice to produce flawless transcripts.

Of course, we thank all the people who took the time to interview with us and whose extensive research and advice helped make *Age Smart* a definitive book on aging well.

"Surgeon to the Stars" Dr. Richard Steadman and "Father of Aerobics" Dr. Kenneth Cooper talked to us about keeping fit at any age. Dr. Cooper, founder of the world-renowned Cooper Aerobics Center, kindly wrote the foreword to this book.

We gained greatly from the collaboration of two other famous doctors, C. Everett Koop, Surgeon General under President Ronald Reagan, and Dr. Louis W. Sullivan, former Secretary of The U.S. Department of Health and Human Services and founding president of the Morehouse School of Medicine.

Renowned scientists and doctors who generously explained their research on aging include Carol Ryff, University of Wisconsin, on stress and social relationships; Giovanni Fava, University of Bologna, on the value of optimism and positive thinking; Janice Kiecolt-Glaser, Ohio State University, on health benefits that marriage provides to men; Michael Irwin, UCLA, on the relationship between exercise, the immune system, and aging; and Cynthia Kenyon, University of California, San Francisco, on genes and aging.

We were lucky enough to speak individually with each member of two legendary American couples. Former President Jimmy Carter and mental health advocate Rosalynn Carter spoke to us about moving through different stages of life and staying active. Helen Gurley Brown, longtime *Cosmopolitan* editor, and her husband, award-winning Hollywood movie producer David Brown, told us their secrets for long and successful marriages and careers.

Leading anthropologists also shared their perspective. Johnnetta Cole, president of Bennett College, discussed staying mentally engaged and relieving stress. Bradd Shore of Emory University helped us put our American ideas about aging in perspective by sharing what he learned from living with the Samoans.

Great businessmen, from vacuum mogul and infomercial superstar David Oreck to Robert Mondavi, founder of Mondavi wineries, shared how they've made success last past the age when most people are long-retired. J.B. Fuqua founded a corporate powerhouse, Fuqua Industries, Truett Cathy is the founder of Chick-fil-A, and Don Keough was the long-term president of the Coca-Cola Company and is now chairman of a leading investment bank, Allen & Co. Dennis Donovan is the executive vice president for human resources at The Home Depot.

We interviewed some inspiring leaders who have been great successes in both sports and business. General Pete Dawkins won the Heisman Trophy playing football for the U.S. Army, and after a distinguished military career, is equally distinguished in business. Roger Staubach won the Heisman Trophy for the U.S. Navy, two Super Bowls as quarterback of the Dallas Cowboys, and went on to found a highly respected real estate firm. Jan Leschly was one of the world's top-ranked tennis players and moved on to a successful second career as the CEO of SmithKline Beecham.

President of *Hearst* Magazines Cathie Black, the "First Lady of American Magazines" and a role model for "sixty as the new forty," shared her thoughts on physical aging. Zig Ziglar showed why he is arguably the world's leading motivational speaker and author. Hilde Gerst, who had built and run an art gallery in New York over many decades, provided a glimpse into how to pursue your passions fearlessly.

Andrew Young is an exemplar of achieving success in multiple careers, as he went from minister to Civil Rights leader to congressman to U.N. Ambassador to Atlanta mayor to promoter of African economic development. Tom Johnson was the president of CNN and is a mentor to the two authors.

Many outstanding people shared their stories of changing careers to find their dreams, and we'd like to thank them all, including those portrayed in the book: Carol Gee, Peter Kastner, Aubrey Garlington, and Carol and Doreen Linneman.

We would also like to thank the Centers for Disease Control experts: Dr. Brad Perkins, Robert N. Anderson, Ph.D., and Elizabeth Arias, Ph.D.

The authors gratefully thank the multitude of friends and contacts who helped us with access to some of the famous people previously mentioned, even at a time when *Age Smart* was just an idea without a publisher. Sean Dawkins, an emerging leader in the financial world who is also a world-class parachutist and skier and Special Forces military veteran, was a driving force and made

ACKNOWLEDGMENTS

his admirable network open to us. We also acknowledge Judy Milestone, Cory Charles, Dr. Bill Amos, the late Bart Herbert, Jonathan Fleming, Michael Drew, Daisy Pareja, Rose Cunningham, Kabhir Sehgal, Terance Fowler, and Dr. Stephen Gerst.

Many friends helped with ideas and suggestions, including Richard Rossi, David Abney, Deepa Nair, Steve Franklin, Doug Buce, Isha Edwards, and Ashley Preisinger.

Of course, we are greatly indebted to our editor, Jim Boyd, and the entire editorial team at Prentice Hall, particularly Kayla Dugger, Russ Hall, and Ginny Munroe for putting their magic touch on the manuscript and keeping us on point. Jim saw the potential in this book and signed us on. He wasn't intimidated by what seemed at first an unwieldy subject matter and instead has steadfastly championed our book through the publishing process despite our sometimes tardy meeting of deadlines. Any editor willing to work with you on deadlines is a writer's dream!

About the Authors

Jeffrey Rosensweig is a finance professor at Emory University. A Ph.D. who studied at MIT and a frequent commentator on national television and at keynote lectures, he studies economic and aging trends and their impact on business and investing strategy. A member of the U.S. Council on Foreign Relations, he resides in Atlanta.

Betty Liu is an anchor on Bloomberg Television and host of the morning program, *Starting Bell*. An award-winning business journalist, Betty has spent the last ten years as a reporter for CNBC, *The Financial Times*, and *Dow Jones Newswires*, covering some of the biggest stories around the world. Raised in Philadelphia, Betty currently resides in New York.

Foreword

I recently received one of the best compliments. A long-time member of our fitness center and Cooper Clinic patient, Fan Benno, wrote me a note after she won a 3,000 meter walking event for women over 85 years of age (she is 87). She wrote, "Because of you, Dr. Cooper, I forgot to grow old." Wouldn't it be nice if we could all forget to grow old?

Not a day goes by when we don't hear about another anti-aging strategy, or a new product or idea that claims to have found the "fountain of youth." No, there is not a magic pill that will instantly make you young, but there is a powerful weapon that when used consistently will let you live a long, full, healthy life—exercise.

A favorite phrase of mine comes from legendary pitcher and humorist Leroy "Satchel" Paige: "How old would you be if you didn't know how old you are?" I could fill pages with examples of people just like Fan who disregard the candles on their birthday cake. One is a 91-year-old man who performs frequently at Cypress Gardens in Florida, waterskiing barefoot on one foot while holding the handle in his mouth. It is impressive to see him whizzing by in all yellow, but even more amazing is that "Banana" George Blair did not start waterskiing until he was past 40 years of age. He even took up a new sport at the age of 75—snowboarding.

"Banana" George is a perfect contradiction to the old adage, "You can't teach an old dog new tricks." Research shows that even moderate activity, when done regularly, can yield major health benefits at any age. The benefits include a reduced risk of chronic diseases, improved mental health, and enhanced physical functioning. Most sedentary people, at any age, who add 30 minutes of physical activity to their day will decrease their body fat and see improvements in their blood pressure, blood glucose, and blood cholesterol. Exercise can counteract muscle weakness and frailty in older individuals, and it delays the onset of disabilities and life-threatening diseases.

I encourage everyone who reads *Age Smart* to look at the other examples of individuals who have not only defied the traditional definition of aging, but embraced a new definition. . . one that does not limit our physical and mental abilities simply by the advancing of years.

And remember, it is fascinating to know that one can grow healthier as one grows older and not necessarily the reverse. Who determines that? You do! To slow down the aging process, eliminate these things: cigarette smoking, inactivity, obesity, and (as much as possible) stress.

Finally, I wish you a long, healthy, and active life, and if you follow these recommendations, I can almost guarantee it.

Dr. Kenneth H. Cooper, M.D., M.P.H
Founder, President, and CEO, Cooper Aerobics Center

Introduction

No matter how young or old you are, one issue will influence how you live, where you'll invest your money, and even what jobs will be available to you. What is it?

It's the aging of America.

Why? As you've probably heard by now, this "aging issue" is a result of the Baby Boomer generation, which consists of tens of millions of babies born between the Second World War (1946) and the Vietnam War (1964). They are the largest swell of people ever born in the United States, and members from this generation have affected everything from our politics (George W. Bush and Bill Clinton) to our cultural tastes (disco and Madonna).

However, it is their sheer size—76 million people—that has, and will have, the greatest impact on your life. By 2030, when all the Baby Boomers have passed traditional retirement age, expectations are that there will be 72 million Americans over the age of 65, nearly double the number of Americans over 65 now (see Appendix, "The Baby Boomer Factor and Life Expectancy," for more analysis of the impact of trends in population and life expectancy). If you think Florida is a crowded place now for retirees, think of how it will be in 25 years!

We aren't just talking about population problems, of course. This doubling of older people has already changed lives in profound ways. If you are part of Generation X (people in their 20s and 30s), you're probably worried that you won't be able to depend on Social Security benefits or Medicare because Baby Boomers will withdraw billions of dollars from the system when they retire.

If you are in your 40s and 50s, you may have already considered a little "nipping and tucking." Thank your fellow Baby

Boomers for making cosmetic procedures—from Botox to face-lifts—common and acceptable.

If you are in your late 60s or 70s and just retired, you're probably thankful you got your benefits *before* your company started slashing pension schemes as management attempts to figure out how to pay for the future Baby Boomer retirees.

It is not all dire straits. The only way you'd be in trouble is if you go on living not knowing this is what is happening in America right here, right now. You cannot change demographic trends. What generation doesn't grow old? But you can change your *reaction* to it, which is precisely why we wrote this book.

Age Smart is about taking aging into your own hands, so you'll be better prepared for whatever demographic or social forces come your way. Whether it is the insolvency of the Social Security system, layoffs at your company, or that at 65, you're still raring to work another 20 years, you'll be in the best shape possible to deal with all of these issues. When we say preparation, we mean every facet of your life: physical, mental, financial, and spiritual.

In our two years of research, one thing we found to be true is how important control—or a sense of control—is to the success of our lives. Makes sense, right? If you're in control, you feel you have some influence over the outcome of events, and that feeling of control makes you feel a bit safer. Even in situations when you have no control—during an illness, for example—researchers have found that those who turned to God or their faith dealt better with their situation because they were at least *controlling their reaction* to the sickness.

Think of *Age Smart* as the guidebook that helps you take *control* of your aging. Of course we don't offer you a way to turn back the clock on those wrinkles or to get the six-pack back in shape. We offer, instead, preparation for aging in the larger sense: preparing your money, your mind, your body, and your career.

From your 30s onward, you have probably asked yourself several times: How do I want to live my life?

Don't think about aging until it is too late, when you've arrived near retirement with a small nest egg and no clear direction about what to do for the next 25 to 35 years of your life. Aging is something you need to think about now because it's happening all around you—and to you.

▪▪▪ Who We Are

The idea for this book came about the way many ideas do: over a meal. We were having a casual lunch with a neurologist who works on innovative new ways to help patients afflicted by Parkinson's disease. He mentioned how recent research confronted long-held beliefs in the medical field that your brain cells die over the course of a lifetime. In fact, he told us that new research shows your brain cells continue to regenerate into your older years, meaning you can still try to stay as mentally sharp at 85 as you were at 35.

As one of us (Jeff) is an economist and the other (Betty) is a financial journalist, we wondered what this nugget of information could mean to Americans who are financially preparing for their retirement. What if everyone knew that they could continue to grow brain cells into their older years? Would people think more seriously about their post-retirement lives if they knew they could stay sharp well into their 80s or 90s? Would they stop thinking of post-65 as a period of utter decline? Would people continue to work well beyond 65? How would working longer affect their nest eggs?

In the same respect, if people knew they could stay mentally acute well into their 80s and beyond, how could they prepare their bodies to match their mental stamina?

We know there are plenty of books out there that discuss aging well as it pertains to health and finances. We used some of these in our own research, such as Dr. Michael Roizen's *Real Age: Are You As Young As You Can Be?* (See the Recommended Sources section in the Appendix for a listing of sources we used and recommend you read.) The problem isn't availability of books on the subject, but that most books tackle the issues of aging well separately.

Aging well, however, isn't about confronting only one area, such as finances or health. It's about handling all areas of your life at the same time, so that they work in harmony. As you'll read in Chapter 8, "Socialize Your Way To Health," learning how having a happy marriage can increase your longevity or how career stress can literally affect your biological system are just some of the ways *Age Smart* approaches the goal of aging well. To live your best life, you must understand how every aspect of your life is interconnected.

Because we couldn't find a book that took a holistic approach to aging smart, we decided to write it ourselves. One of us (Jeff) has been lecturing for years around the country about the "Baby Boomer effect" on the U.S. economy, and the other (Betty) has been writing about social and economic trends for the past 10 years as a reporter with *The Financial Times* and other major news organizations.

Both of us put our vast resources together to find the latest research and advice to help you prepare for your future. As one of us is a Baby Boomer and the other a Generation Xer, we were intensely curious on our own accord to try to find out how to optimize living well into our 50s, 60s, 70s, and beyond.

▪▪▪ Our Research

As noted earlier, this book is the culmination of two years of research. Both of us sifted through thousands of pages of medical research and articles to bring you the latest and most proven ways to help you gain longevity.

We tapped into the expertise of doctors at the world-renowned Cleveland Clinic, and we were also able to easily access the nation's leading doctors through Jeff's advisory work with PinnacleCare International, a service that helps link member clients with the world's top physicians.

The research for this book, however, went beyond just reading the latest articles. We headed straight to the leading thinkers and researchers in the medical field to get their advice and views on aging well. You'll read some of these interviews later in the book, such as with Dr. C. Everett Koop, the former U.S. Surgeon General, and Dr. Louis W. Sullivan, founder of the Morehouse School of Medicine and former Secretary of The U.S. Department of Health and Human Services.

As with most research, we interviewed far more people than included by name in the book, from scientists and doctors at the National Institutes of Health to sociologists and gerontologists at the University of Michigan and Cornell. We interviewed economists, anthropologists, and psychologists to get their expertise on aging well. We even spoke with leaders at Fortune 500 companies, such as Dennis Donovan at the Home Depot, to see how the "older worker" is changing and benefiting businesses.

We also wanted to go beyond "experts" to talk to real people who have aged fabulously to find out their secrets. Some of the more famous people we interviewed for the book include former President Jimmy Carter and his wife, Rosalynn, and Helen Gurley Brown and her husband, director David Brown. We also spoke with ordinary people who lead extraordinary lives and who remain active well into their 80s and 90s. What have they done to age so well and how can we tap into their "secrets"? We talked to organizations, such as *Discovering What's Next*, to find out what happens as people discover new careers beyond retirement.

We also analyzed the latest data and economic trends to help guide your finances through your 30s, 40s, 50s, and older. As you'll find out later, some of the financial advice is contrary to what you've been told by financial planners and advisers for years (because many of them expect you to practically roll over and die after age 65).

Ultimately, we hope this book will both inform and inspire you to look forward to your older years. Frankly speaking, the secrets to a long and healthy life boil down to very simple things: eat right, get consistent aerobic exercise, get plenty of rest, be happy, have a purpose, and keep everything in moderation. How you do these things requires far more complexity and motivation on your part. With that in mind, *Age Smart* was written to make it a little easier for you to live a long, healthy, and prosperous life.

CHAPTER

1

Just Say No to Pink Pants

A number of years ago, Donald Keough, president of Coca-Cola, retired. At 66, this garrulous, hard-charging, oft-described "people-person" executive was reluctant to leave, but he had reached the mandatory retirement age. Most of his friends and colleagues, as would be expected, thought he would walk into the sunset with his pockets full of cash to enjoy devoted family time. He would lead the retirement life so many people dream about—rich, abundant in energy, and free of worries. So, on a cool Friday morning in Spring, Don packed up his office, bade goodbye to his colleagues, and made his graceful exit.

But by Monday, much to the surprise of his friends, Don flew to New York to take a job chairing a boutique investment bank called Allen & Co. "Don, what are you doing?" his friends asked, perplexed. Don was a man with many millions of dollars who could do anything he wanted—join some boards, travel the world, and build his dream house or houses. But Don wanted to work again. Hard work. "You've been working *all* your life," another friend declared, who seemed more puzzled by the move than happy for him. "Why don't you relax for a bit and then jump back in?"

"You kidding?" Don replied to each of the inquiring friends. "I'd end up like those guys in pink pants."

As Don later told us when we interviewed him, he'd been vacationing for many years at an exclusive coastal golf resort. The place was Palm Springs meets Southern hospitality. Most people were retirees from the upper echelons of society, spending their days enjoying the beaches and golf courses, dining at world-famous restaurants, and driving their yachts out onto the sapphire-blue water. To you and me, it would be Retiree Utopia. But for Don, it was Retiree Prison.

Over the years, he'd begun to realize this happy place was inhabited by some unhappy people. Every time he visited, invariably one or two friends or acquaintances would tug at his sleeve and take him aside. "Don," they'd breathe. "What's it like out there in the *real world?*"

"What do you mean?"

"You know, the real world. The place where things happen, where you've got a place to be, people to meet. I'm going crazy here with all this time on my hands. I never thought I'd say it, but I need to get *away* from this." *This*, of course, meaning a permanent "dream" retirement.

The one thing Don noticed about these people was that many of them wore pink pants. Or pink shorts. Some pants were more of a pastel pink. Others wore salmon-colored pants. One sported generous flamingo pink neon. "There's something about when you go into retirement and spend a few years in that phase of life, that suddenly all these perfectly well-dressed men start wearing these God-awful pink pants. I said to myself, I said to my wife, I will never be caught dead in those damn pink pants."

That was how Don decided his second act was going to be as far away from the golf resort as possible. At 79, he's as energetic as ever, jetting across the globe to meetings, overseeing corporate mergers that you and I have probably read about in the newspapers, and mentoring the next generation of corporate leaders and CEOs. Rather than pink pants, he has stayed in his favorite business suits.

Don's story describes a lot of what this book is about. It's about throwing out all conceptions about the traditional retirement years. It's about defying the conventions that say aging means a bland, low-excitement life. It's about how to prepare *now*—financially, physically, mentally—for your second or even third act.

It's about saying no to wearing pink pants.

▪▪▪ Aging Is Not a Dirty Word

Age Smart is about aging well, not staying young.

Staying young is something Hollywood does, presenting ageless beauties and hunks who look better at age 45 than at 25. That's not what we are talking about. We think that's unhealthy for a variety of reasons, but mostly because to look the way Tom Cruise or Demi Moore does requires *a lot* of money and trainers.

You probably know of many people who personify the "no pink pants" ideal. Here are just a few:

- Millionaire and extreme adventurer, Steve Fossett, who set a world record for flying solo nonstop across the globe at the age of 60.
- President George Bush, Sr., who dove out of an airplane to celebrate his 80th birthday.
- Soul legend, Tina Turner, who slid back into her high heels to start an exhausting world tour at the age of 65.
- Clint Eastwood, who won his third Oscar for *Million Dollar Baby*, proving that he is amazingly doing his best work at the age of 74.
- Ruth Bader Ginsburg, who is the last remaining woman on the powerful Supreme Court and who entered 2006 at age 72, having served 12 years on the top court.
- Joe Paterno, who coached Penn State over Florida State in the Orange Bowl in January 2006 at age 79. (Interestingly, Florida State was coached by the "young" Bobby Bowden, age 76!)

Growing older is not what it used to be. It's better. Newspaper and magazine articles loudly proclaim "Sixty is the new forty" or that "Seventy is the new fifty." Whatever you like. But the truth is that people *really* are living richer, fuller lives in their later years, thanks to all sorts of advances in the medical field—from blood pressure medications, to new knees, to better health monitoring. We're eating healthier, despite the justified obesity concerns.

We're smoking less. We're more environmentally concerned. It's all adding up to an improved quality of life. I bet if we asked you to name at least one or two people who are active, passionate, don't-look-their-age seniors, you'd be able to name them in a second. Perhaps they are your own parents, grandparents, an aunt, or a friend's father. These are people who appear to defy the odds—and surprisingly, there are plenty of people out there who are just like them.

Does Everyone Hate Getting Old?

We asked that question of Bradd Shore, a colleague of ours and a professor in anthropology at Emory University who happens to be one of the leading cultural observers in this country and lectures around the world. For decades, Dr. Shore has closely studied the Samoans, a tribal people in the South Pacific.

Yes and no was his answer. "To some extent, aging isn't fun anywhere," he says. "When you talk to people about aging, even in societies like Samoa where they have a place for old people, old people would still rather be young than old."

But he did find one marked difference in his extensive observation of Samoans in terms of aging. "What I discovered in Samoa was that they have two different conceptions of power. One is *pule power,* which is direct authority over people. The other kind is *mana,* which is a passive power, the power you get by sitting. It's associated with withdrawal from activity. The highest-ranking chiefs were understood to be sitting chiefs.

"Their understanding of the life course for people is that life moves from the young to increasing energy in middle life, and then the energy reverses in your older years. The difference is that for Americans, that's associated with losing something because you're no longer active. Samoans have this notion that we sit now, sit back and gain in dignity. The value of inactivity is accorded a positive status."

In our ambitious, fast-paced culture, it's hard to imagine anyone accepting that sort of life trajectory and becoming just a sitting power head; however, Dr. Shore does have a point that being old, or even older, is often denigrated in our society. Aging is often associated with being plain old useless.

"I'm going to turn 60 next month and periodically I find myself saying, now remember, think like a Samoan, every age has its positives," says Dr. Shore. "My mother visited Samoa several times—the last time she went she was 78. She went there and the nice Samoan family taking care of her always referred to her as an old lady. She said, 'Why do they keep calling me an old lady?' I said, 'Well what else are you? They're not calling you a name; they're addressing you by your status.' She had to stop and realize that this was a positive thing."

"I don't try to look like I'm 20," Dr. Shore adds, with a laugh. "But my [observation] of the Samoans has made the process of aging a little easier. I'm not afraid of less activity. I'll have a different type of status. My idea is not to try to be young but to try to find the best version of who I am and to let that happen."

What we're proposing in this book isn't a post-retirement life plan or a plan for what to do after you reach age 65. It's a life plan that *prepares* you for your post-65 period. That's a big difference. What can you do right now—in your 30s, 40s, 50s, 60s, and beyond—to ensure your life is vibrant and dynamic up until the very end?

We show you that achieving this is not dumb luck. Clint Eastwood isn't "lucky" to be working at 74—he most likely practiced for this vibrancy his whole life. He might not have done everything right, but we're pretty sure that staying involved in directing movies—a huge intellectual undertaking—helps him age well by challenging his brain. That doing this comes to him naturally is a gift, but it's certainly not exclusive to him. If we all mentally challenge ourselves throughout our lives, we'll have a much better chance of aging well.

Luckily for Clint, he doesn't need to worry about his finances. But chances are, you do. A goal of our life plan is to help you in *all* aspects. Aging well is not just about preserving your body, exercising your brain, or making sure your retirement nest egg is enough. It's about integrating *all those things*. Just as exercising does wonders for your brain, plenty of savings can do wonders for your peace of mind and happiness. We don't compartmentalize daily living—we are not file cabinets in which we can access each part of our lives when we feel like it.

Money, health, happiness—all these things come tumbling at us in waves, jumbled together like seaweed.

We take all this into account as we construct a guide for you to age well and age smart. We've also added in real-life stories from people who live like Clint—smart, savvy, and incredibly active at a time when most think they should be heading to the nursing home. People who age well and smart are true followers of "no pink pants." We hope you'll learn a thing or two from them or just enjoy reading about their experiences.

First, we want to tell you a little more about the dirty little word—"aging"—and why it's so important you know as much about it as possible.

▪▪▪ A Look at the Dirty Word

From the time you turned 21, you probably began to realize that you're not growing up any longer, you're growing *older*. Maybe it was that first job out of college. Or suddenly, you found you couldn't sprint quite as fast as you did when you were in high school, but heck, you're still doing a lot better than those 30-year-olds out on the basketball court.

Then, you turned 30. And gosh, the clock was suddenly set on fast forward—every minute meant another drop in the bucket, and that bucket was sure filling fast. If you're a woman, you gave a double-take when fresh-faced waiters started calling you "ma'am." If you're a guy, your heart might have fluttered when you looked in the bathroom mirror and saw some *thinning* going on up there. Aging becomes a *race*, a sprint against that cruel dimension called Time, and deep down, you always know that Time will win. But regardless, you pile on the face and body products, you try to hit the gym, you down vitamins upon vitamins, you even go into denial. "I don't feel my age at all! I feel 25!"

The joke, it seems, is that by the time you've come to terms with aging, you're already too old. When you are young and vibrant, you don't really want to settle with the idea that you are going through *senescence*—the gradual deterioration of body parts. We think that somehow we can stay 25 forever. Could this be the reason why a majority of Americans are still completely unprepared financially for retirement? Could this also be behind the fact that more than 60 percent of us don't regularly exercise? Is it why plastic surgery is more common among people over 50?

Why do we age? Why can't we be like sea anemones that live indefinitely (barring some awful accident, such as a whale chomping it into bits)? Or why can't we stay 11 years old, the age when our regenerative capacity is strongest? Some scientists figure that if we maintained 11-year-old bodies throughout our lives, we could live 1,200 years, barring any significant diseases or accidents!

It could be that aging is Mother Nature's way of urging us to reproduce. Imagine a world in which nobody aged. Would we delay having children or not even bother at all? Think of the problems if Grandpa decided he wanted to keep working forever, thereby creating a log jam of employees as each generation matures. Scientists experimenting with caloric restriction on animals and insects—one of the proven ways to slow aging— have found almost all the subjects invariably lose their ability to *reproduce*. Or at least, their fertility is vastly diminished.

Aging is one of the least understood processes in science. That doesn't mean there aren't some perfectly sensible and likely theories, and very possibly you've heard one or two. Like the theory that our cells get hit over time by oxygen radicals (oxidants) that eventually damage our organs (which is why you hear so much about eating foods rich in anti-oxidants). Or that our genes control aging, switching on and off sequentially through the course of our lives. Even just the conventional "wear and tear" theory, which hypothesizes we're built like machines whose vital parts eventually just wear out and die. Nobody knows for sure what causes aging.

The Worm Lady

Genes, schmenes. Although aging is largely not under our control, we know that some powerful possibilities to extend our lives are locked up in our genetic fiber. It's just a matter of finding them.

Some of the most exciting genetic research has come out of Dr. Cynthia Kenyon's lab at the University of California, San Francisco. She largely accelerated genetic research into aging when she published findings back in 1993 that noted altering certain genes in microscopic C. Elegans worms helped them live twice as long—and remain in good shape.

"If you showed these worms to someone, they'd think they were probably five days old, when in reality, they are 10 or 15 days old," she explained in a recent interview. "It's the same as looking at an 80-year-old and thinking he's 40."

Dr. Kenyon and her work have been portrayed not only in science journals, but also in leading weekly news magazines. One of the few leading female geneticists, she altered the worms' genes by controlling an insulin-like hormone system that when suppressed, helps kick-start a protein called DAF-16, which binds to anti-aging genes and flicks them on like a light switch. The result? Longer-living worms that are dating and playing tennis long after their normal peers have shriveled up and died.

Since her initial discovery, others have found that these hormones also control the aging of mammals: changing the genes in mice extends their lifespan, too. What's more, the same changes that extend lifespan also delay many age-related diseases, such as cancer and heart disease. The genes, when inhibited, not only slow down aging, but also protect the organism from harmful environmental effects like UV exposure. In effect, the more we know about genes and how they work, the more we realize it's not about finding one or two "anti-aging" genes, but about understanding how our entire complex body monitors and repairs itself. The interesting thing is that the whole network seems to be controlled by single genes that act as master-regulators. So, if people turn out to be like mice and worms, it may be possible one day to pop a pill and stay young a little while longer.

We may not even have to wait for a pill. Dr. Kenyon, who's learned a thing or two herself from these worms, told us that red wine contains resveratrol, an anti-oxidant that activates a protein, SIR-2, that also ironically kicks DAF-16 into gear. "The increase [to your lifespan] might be about 10 to 15 percent, so don't get too excited," she says. "But you see, the point is, it may already exist. There's already ways that we can tap into these control systems that control aging."

What has Dr. Kenyon learned for herself? "I put on sunscreen every day, right out of the shower," she says. She follows a "low-glycemic index" diet—meaning she stays away from simple starches and sugars, which helps keep her insulin levels low and stable. "I don't eat sweets or potatoes or pasta or rice," she says. "I did this research with the worms and immediately, I switched my diet."

Just because we don't know exactly why we age doesn't mean aging is a hopeless endeavor. In fact, aging is something we have surprising control over. There are things you can do right here and right now that will help play the odds in your favor between a short and suffering life or a youthful and vibrant one.

Think that your life span is *primarily* determined by what you do from the moment you are born. Your genes, though incredibly powerful and complex, account for roughly 30 percent of how long you'll live. The rest is up to you.

We owe much to our genes, but it's really the environment that creates who we are, how long we live, and whether we die at 55 from a heart attack or at 102 peacefully in our beds. Incredibly enough, as our knowledge of genetics grows, we see ever more clearly how *small* a role genes play in our development.

Take diseases. Contrary to what most people think, people are not involved in a game of Russian roulette by which cancer or coronary heart disease strikes at random moments. Even for people with the Type 1 diabetes gene and who possess a family history of diabetes, the probability of developing the disease is only 25 percent. Think of it the other way—you have the genetic predisposition, your family has a history, and you still have a 75 percent chance of *never* getting Type 1 diabetes. Whether you develop the disease depends *entirely* on how you live. Think if we told you that for the rest of your life, you'd have a 75 percent chance of winning the lottery. You'd probably stop by the 7-Eleven store every day after work to buy a ticket, wouldn't you? The odds are *that* good. The same goes for your health and aging well. What you do now will make a huge difference later on. It's not about Lady Luck. It's about being diligent and taking care of your body, mind, and soul so that you fall on the right side of the odds.

▪▪▪ Good Humor and Other Things

When most of us think of aging, we think of our body and health and our retirement. We worry about whether we are taking care of our bodies. Are we eating the right foods? Are we exercising enough? Are we going to develop crow's feet or age spots?

We also worry if we're socking enough money away for the post-65 retirement period. Do we have enough to sustain our way of life for the next 20 or 30 years? How much should we save? What are the best retirement accounts?

When it comes to aging well, most of the books and magazine articles focus on getting these two areas on track—health and retirement. They should—these areas are of utmost importance as we look toward our future. But they're not the *only* things we should look at when we think of aging well.

We don't often think about whether having an unhappy marriage is cutting our lives short. Or whether the stress we feel from work is slowly making us susceptible to heart disease, cancer, and other chronic diseases (not to mention adding plenty of wrinkles and bags under the eyes). Or that staying curious is one way to exercise the mind, protecting against Alzheimer's and other forms of dementia.

When Jean Calment died in Arles, France at the age of 122, she became the longest living human being on record. Over the years of her life, scientists discussed her diet and her exercise routine, observed her living conditions, and recorded her mental acuity. But rarely did anyone talk about her great sense of humor. Ms. Calment once told a story about a lawyer who signed her up for a pension scheme that gave her monthly payments in exchange for the ownership of her apartment. Being that Ms. Calment was already 90 back in 1965, it appeared the deal was a win for the lawyer—he'd only have to make a few payments before she died and the company could seize ownership. But not only did Ms. Calment live for another 32 years, she also outlived the lawyer and received payments worth three times the value of her apartment! To which the French lady quipped once, "We all make bad deals in life." In another story, a reporter said at Ms. Calment's 120th birthday party that he'd "see her next year," eliciting the feisty centenarian to reply, "I don't see why not. You look to be in pretty good health to me!"

Ms. Calment's sense of humor was likely an important factor in her living to 122, just as what she ate or how much she exercised. But you never hear much about that.

Things that have a clear cause-effect relationship are easy to understand. If you smoke, you can get lung cancer. If you eat too many French fries, you'll likely get fat. If you don't save at least 10 percent of your paychecks, you'll be less prepared for retirement.

How do you evaluate the concrete health benefits of being able to see the funny things in life, as Ms. Calment could? Or being religious? Or being a happy person? Or having a happy marriage? It's not as if you can say, "Laugh three times a day to lessen your chance of heart disease."

Thankfully, an increasing amount of research is devoted to just these topics, melding the fields of psychology, neurology, epidemiology, and sociology. Some have pinpointed how many years an unhappy marriage might lop off your life, or exactly what happens to people biologically after they've attended church regularly. We present some of the most exciting research in this book, along with interviews from some of the leading doctors around the country.

Science is sort of playing catch-up because in many ways, there are millions of people in this country who are aging well and practicing the "aging secrets" that are just now being corroborated by research. People who've reached their 70s, 80s, and 90s intrinsically know what's made them live so long—and it's not just about diet and exercise. Phil Mazzilli, a vibrant 95-year-old retired property assessor who worked up until two years ago, confesses his diet for his whole life has been "off color." Instead, he attributes his long life to not letting stress wear him out.

"I never ate greens. I didn't like salads. My favorite meal was sausage with a pepper wedge," he admits. "People who have stomach troubles, it's not from what you eat, it's from your nerves. Everything reacts to nerves. You worry about this or that, worry about not doing anything right, that'll get you. As it stands now, I've done very well for myself; I'm content and satisfied. When I go, I go. I'm not going to worry about it."

Aging well is a central issue right now because for the first time in all of humanity, a majority of people on average will live to old ages. We talk more about life expectancies and the Baby Boomer generation later in the book, but just think that only a mere 100 years ago, most Americans could expect to live only until their 40s. That doesn't mean there weren't elderly people in previous generations—George Washington lived to the ripe old age of 67, outlasting a typical American man of his time by about 15 years. But average Americans had a short, often hard life.

Then with better sanitation, the development of vaccines and antibiotics, and improved living conditions, Americans suddenly saw their life expectancies jump as babies stopped dying shortly after birth. Improving medical care and health prevention measures—like raising public awareness about the dangers of smoking and not wearing seat belts—lifted life expectancies from birth even further in 2003 to 75 years for men and to 80 years for women.

We're cresting right now. Any further gains we make in extending our lives are going to come either out of someone's genetic lab or out of us practicing a better lifestyle. Being that any miracle life-extending drugs are probably decades, if not centuries, away, aging well now is a matter of doing a bunch of things that add up to the *one big thing*: a long and healthy life.

Even people on the cutting edge of longevity research know that for now, aging well is a matter of practicing simple habits, such as getting enough sleep, keeping stress down, and having good, strong relationships. Jonathan Fleming, one of the country's leading biotechnology venture capitalists, recognizes that with all the money poured into genetic research, with grand plans of finding the magic life-extending gene or genes, one of the greatest inventions in recent years to lengthen people's lives boils down to something as basic as an artificial joint. Fleming says:

This has been a revolution [in longevity] because the biggest risk to mortality as you age is falling. If you fall and break your hip, you can get complications from a broken hip and that can lead to death. Now you've got grandmas living to be 90 years old with robot parts in them. It's incredible. It's the shift that makes it possible for your golden years to be 30 years long.

▪▪▪ Three Things You Can Do Now to Live Longer

Let's start by discussing three things you can do now to live well and live longer.

Reduce stress! Recent research has found that the effects of stress may be much more ominous than previously thought. Stress may very well be the single factor between living a healthy and long life or a miserable and stunted one. Stress is not just something that wears us down and makes our muscles tighten up; it actually changes our *internal biological systems.*

Take just one system—the immune system. Studies have found that chronic stress, such as the kind endured by taking care of someone with Alzheimer's disease, increases the level of cytokines called Interleukin-6. Normally, the IL-6 cytokines are good for you. Think of cytokines as proteins that act like little traffic cops, directing immune-responsive cells to places where you've been infected or injured. The IL-6 traffic cops help promote inflammation, a beneficial reaction as you deal with infection and trauma.

The problem is that when you're not injured or infected, you don't want these extra guys coursing through your body. They start whistling for these pro-inflammatory cells that have nowhere to go and pretty soon, you have a low-grade buzz of inflammation. Chronic inflammation is bad for you. It promotes muscle weakness. Studies found patients with elevated levels of IL-6 were more likely to be disabled later on because their muscles atrophied easier. Stressed patients with higher levels of IL-6 in their bodies had a harder time absorbing the full effects of a flu vaccine, making them more at risk for infection. Their bodies also took longer to heal from wounds. Chronic inflammation is linked to osteoporosis, cancer, diabetes, and arthritis. That's why your dentist is always looking out for gingivitis—you don't want a low-grade buzz of inflammation because it can cause a whole host of problems.

Stress, whether temporary or chronic, suppresses the body's defenses against infection and malignant growth. It makes you at risk for diseases down the road. You can eat oat bran for breakfast and run five miles a day, but if you're stressed out, you're not getting the full benefits of eating right and exercising.

Scientists aren't sure why stress elevates these IL-6 cytokines, thereby creating this chronic state of inflammation. But they do know that as you age, your ability to regulate these cytokines is diminished. It's much easier for them to go wayward when you're stressed.

Your job is not only to go get a massage every time you feel your shoulders tighten, but to also think about getting rid of or blocking the *chronic stress* before it happens. We're talking big changes. Perhaps you need to learn to be a more optimistic person, therefore allowing you to cope better with challenges.

Or maybe you need to get out of an unhappy relationship. Or maybe you need to prepare for long-term care for your parents. These are the things that will matter for your health as much as exercising and eating right.

It's incredible to think that stress, which isn't something you can touch or see, can wreak such havoc on your body. We dive into more detail later about other ways stress can affect your body, including causing declines in natural killer cells and creating what researchers call an "allostatic load" that makes you more susceptible to diseases.

But for now, make it a commitment to reduce stress in your life. Think of it not just as creating a happier you, but also as a way of adding years to your life.

The older you are, the healthier you'll be? Most people fear growing older because they're worried about developing diseases that will ravage their bodies and minds. The statistics can be frightening—after age 40, your chance of developing chronic illnesses increases dramatically. Health screenings become more important than ever. Chances are, by the time you've reached 50 or so, you'll probably know several close friends who've been diagnosed with cancer, suffered a heart attack, or developed diabetes. Or maybe it will be you.

There is a bright side to this. Each year that passes disease-free increases your chances of living longer in the future. It's what statisticians call *conditional life expectancy*—the number of years *more* you'll live based on your current age. Remember that life expectancy now for a man in America is 75 years. That's at birth— just out of the starting gate. Consider that if you're a man and you've reached age 50 in good shape, your life expectancy is actually going to increase more than three years to 78.5. If you're lucky or smart and hit 65 in good condition, you'll likely reach nearly 82! The news is just as good for women; if you reach 65, you're likely going to outlive your man by three years.

Rather than dread reaching, say, age 65, you should be proud of it. That means you've just given yourself a huge chance to make it to 80 without any major problems. Ditto for reaching 85. Or 90. Or beyond. It's the people who hit 50 and suffer a heart attack that have to worry. If you're 75 and having a ball, you've got it made.

Some scientists link this phenomenon to James Fries' "compression of morbidity" hypothesis, which basically theorizes that as you reach the upper limits of your lifespan, diseases tend to be compressed to the last years of life. In other words, if you haven't developed diabetes by 65, chances are that you are not going to develop it until you're very, very, very old. Or maybe not at all. People studying centenarians who carry the APOE4 gene for Alzheimer's find that the risk of developing the disease falls dramatically after age 85. That's right; the older the patients are, the less likely they'll get dementia! If the patient hasn't developed it before 85, chances are pretty slim he'll develop it later, even if he *carries* the gene.

Your goal is not to get depressed with each birthday, but to celebrate the passing of another year. A birthday just means you've given yourself one more extension to live a longer and healthier life. Celebrate it!

If you want to age well, it is best to live in the U.S. or another wealthy nation. You've already done something wonderful for your longevity if you live in this country.

Sometimes, we take for granted that life expectancies are going up because we have access to a lot of medicine, clean water, flushing toilets, and well-stocked supermarkets. In other parts of the world, such as Africa, life expectancy is still a short 37 to 45 years because of violence, conflict, food shortages, poor sanitation, lack of access to clean water, and diseases such as AIDS. In Russia, life expectancy *reversed* course between 1989 and 1994 for men, falling seven years, owing to homicide, drugs, poor diet, and alcoholism.

Even with all we have access to, we're not number one in terms of life expectancy. Other countries, such as Japan, France, Norway, and Italy have longer living people, and it is there we've tried to find the secrets to aging well. Is it their diets? Their exercise regimes? Their culture? We're still trying to figure it out.

Living in America gives us some fundamental tools to help us reach old age gracefully. The U.S. has great medical care. Americans have plenty of material possessions, which though they don't directly make us live longer, *do* offer us a more comfortable living. We have access to the finest education in the world, an important aspect to aging well.

Most importantly, we have control over our lives, which makes a huge difference in how well we age. In the exhaustive, 10-year landmark study funded by the MacArthur Foundation, "Midlife in the U.S.," researchers found that control "was associated with better health and well-being for adults of all ages." Americans have the freedom to age the way they want to—in some other countries without free societies, the concept of "aging well" is not really an option.

Remember that over 70 percent of the aging process is under your control. Having control can make a world of difference in your life and how well you age. Imagine if you didn't have any control over your aging—and think about how lucky you are that we do.

Taking control of aging means tackling each section of your life and making sure it's in the best possible condition: your body, your money, your mind, and, for lack of a better word, your soul. These separate areas of your life work in concert as you age. Your job is to make sure they are primed. If you do this, you give yourself the best chance to live a happy, healthy, and long life.

▄▄ David Oreck: Still Selling Vacuums At 81

Turn on your television set and sooner or later, you'll see an infomercial featuring an energetic man with Bassett Hound eyes imploring you to take the "Oreck Challenge." That's the 30-day, risk-free trial that has helped make David Oreck's vacuum cleaners a household name.

It's hard to believe David Oreck is 81 years old. He drives his Harley Davidson motorcycles to work. On his days off, he flies planes on his farm near New Orleans. (He flew bomber missions in Japan during World War II.) He walks or runs several miles a day. And he's still the face behind the Oreck vacuums he made famous by creating them both powerful and *light*.

Ever the consummate salesman, David Oreck spends part of his time—when not hawking his vacuum cleaners—traveling around the country inspiring people to reach for their dreams at any age. David himself is a perfect example—he didn't start his company until he was 40. Today, David Oreck has sold millions of vacuum cleaners around the world and is lauded for his vision in helping revolutionize home cleaning.

David Oreck is someone who has aged smart by demonstrating success and fulfillment can begin at any age. He is just one of the several people we've interviewed who proves that life can be just as fast in your 80s as in your 20s—with a few limits, of course!

I'm in pretty good health for my age. I'm still vertical in other words. I guess I've always been busy and never really known anything different. It's very good for you to be busy and I kind of think if I were to retire as some people do, I'd go downhill.

I used to run a lot. I don't run thousands of miles anymore because I realized I wasn't getting anywhere. When you run, the knees and back go first. But I am active every day, and being involved keeps you going right along. In New Orleans, the weather makes it walkable outside at times, but we have pretty hot summers. I get used to that.

I'm not a big drinker. I didn't drink for 15 years and then I got married 8 years ago, remarried I should say, and on the occasion of the wedding, I had a glass of champagne. It was the first taste of any alcohol that I'd had for 15 years and it tasted awfully good. So about 8 years ago, I resumed moderate drinking. Sometimes, I take a "big boy" drink, such as a martini.

I never thought about aging at all. I just didn't. I didn't think I was necessarily bullet proof. It astounds me every time I give my age because I don't feel that age. I don't think that way. People always think I'm blowing blue smoke at them because I don't act my age. I don't deny myself anything. I go out when I feel like it, and I stay out as late as I feel like. I work out or fly or whatever. I don't feel as if I'm denying myself anything. Fortunately, we're successful, and if I was unsuccessful, I might not have the same attitude. The company is doing well and I know I make a meaningful contribution. We have very good people here, my son is president of the company, and he takes over a lot of the nitty-gritty areas of things, such as marketing. I'm sure that if life were tougher, I'm sure that would take its toll.

I've always worked hard. I haven't always been successful. Every large company was once a small company and even in the company today, I'm still picking up paper clips I see on the floor. A lot of people don't do that and that ticks me off a bit. They didn't start from zero and I did. I didn't start my company until I was 40 years of age. I talk to a lot of universities around the country. I've talked to more than 40—I was just at Harvard on Valentine's Day—and the thing I tell to young people, the point I always make, is that I didn't get my start in this business until I was 40. A lot of young people get encouragement from that because they don't know anybody, and they have no connections and no money or financial backing. When you think about it, Henry Ford was in his 60s before he made his millions.

I'm the oldest guy here. I'm not the only guy who's up there a bit, but we have low turnover in this company, younger people included, and we don't have a policy for retirement. When I'm gone, they'll probably put one in. But I don't think we should. As long as a guy is productive, he's valuable. My personal feeling in business is if I could hire a guy 60 years of age, who had a good background and is in reasonably good health, that is a fantastic asset to be able to get all that experience from someone who wants to work. That kind of guy is terrific. It's true that he may not be good for more than 5 or 10 years, or whatever that might be, but I would rather have one good year out of an outstanding guy than 10 years from one who's not so good.

Typically, I get up at 5:00 or 5:30 a.m. and work out for an hour and a half. I'll read some papers and catch up on the news a bit. I get to work around 9:30—I used to be here at 8:00, but now I indulge myself. I'll work at the mail, getting all that out of the way. I get voluminous amounts of mail, some of it is fan mail. I want people to know we're approachable, we care, we produce a good product, and we stand behind it. I can't answer all the mail, but I answer a lot of it. I take as many calls as I can, and I read every letter of complaint that comes on my desk and see to it that someone does something about it. Sometimes, I'll attend some meetings that are important, and I spend a fair amount of time on the phone with our creative people.

I generally leave here at about 6:30 or 7:00 p.m. I still have a pretty long day, but I don't mind. The day goes pretty fast. I no longer have two-martini lunches, not even one. We travel a lot, so if I'm in New York, I'll go to the theatre. I go to bed fairly early these days, and generally, I watch the news on TV before dozing off. I don't need a sleeping pill. I just turn the TV on, put the timer on that damn thing, and I'm gone before it's off . . . unless I'm out partying. Now that's another story.

YOUR BODY

CHAPTER

2

No Excuses! Exercising Is Key to Staying Young

Why is it so hard for people to exercise? The Centers for Disease Control reports that 60 percent of adults don't regularly exercise, meaning adults don't spend even 30 minutes a day getting their heart rate pumping. Even worse, a quarter of American adults—that's roughly 55 million people—don't exercise at all. Yet, an average American spends four hours—*four hours!*—a day in front of the television.

So it's not for lack of time.

Exercise is grueling. It takes work. We *know* how hard it is to drag ourselves to the gym after a 10-hour workday. We *know* it's good for us. We *know* it helps our heart, our mental health, and our mood. We *know* it's one of the best ways to lose weight. We *know* that exercise can prevent diseases. So why do we choose not to do it?

Maybe that's the problem. We think of exercise as a choice. We think of it as something to do outside of our daily routines.

Maybe we should start thinking of exercise as a non-negotiable part of our lives. Cathie Black, the president of Hearst Magazines, told us that the day she started exercising regularly was the day she changed her thinking about exercising. She began to regard it the same as a meeting or appointment. She scheduled it in. Instead of breakfast meetings, Cathie penned in exercise.

According to the American Society for Aesthetic Plastic Surgery, people 51 years old and over represent more than 70 percent of the face and forehead lifts done in this country. Men and women over 65 are one of the fastest growing segments of the plastic surgery clientele; they accounted for 6 percent of all plastic surgeries in 2004. And by 2005, Americans will have spent almost $42 billion on anti-aging medicine.

Cathie Black: First Lady of Magazines

Cathleen "Cathie" Black is a true powerhouse in the worlds of business and publishing. The leading global newspaper, *The Financial Times*, recently dubbed her "The First Lady of American Magazines" and "one of the leading figures in American publishing over the past two decades." She is president of Hearst Magazines, the world's largest publisher of monthly magazines. She is in charge of some of the industry's most popular titles: *Cosmopolitan; Popular Mechanics; Esquire; Good Housekeeping; Marie Claire; O, The Oprah Magazine; Redbook; Town and Country*—21 in all. She also oversees 137 international editions of these magazines in more than 100 nations.

What does a woman who publishes magazines to a mostly young female audience have to say about aging?

I started realizing I would turn 60. It's different than 50. You're at a different life stage clearly. Many years ago, for Gloria Steinem's birthday, she sent out an invitation with a picture of herself and she's very pretty, and it said, "This is what 40 looks like." And it was to celebrate her birthday. I think if you have that life attitude, that makes a big difference. We grew up in a generation where a grandparent turning 40, well, it was practically over. But if you are a professional person and you live in the media world, part of what I do, my presence, how I look, is important. I put time and effort into looking good because I want people to say wow, that's what 60 can look like.

I don't think I have ever feared aging. There are people who are very frightened of it, and too often, there are people who don't have other meaningful compartments of their lives that are filled with things other than their work or probably "looks." I have a colleague who is a beautiful woman who decided a few years ago to knock five years off her life, to say that she was five years younger or more—seven, actually. I said, "What are you, crazy? Why would you do that?" She's married and has children, but it's just bizarre.

People always say to me "Gee, you look like you lost weight" and for me, I internalize that in a negative way. My whole family is built just the way I am, tall and slender. About four years ago, maybe even five, I would run in Central Park, two or three times a week, but never any distance, just to really sort of stay fit.

And I remember I heard Ann Richards, the former governor of Texas, talking about osteoporosis. She then went on to do a book about it. In her family, there's a strain of osteoporosis, and she had gotten to a point where she was having a lot of difficulty. So she went on an exercise regime and was so proud of herself because she'd done some huge walk with her daughter in Texas. She said that a year before there was no way she could have done it. For some reason, that was a click for me. I thought to myself, I am now going to make exercise a priority. Because she was doing this whole thing on upper body, and too many women do no upper body development. I said to myself, "I'm going to make a stronger commitment to get fit than I'd ever done before. I'm going to get a trainer, and I'm going to make that more important than another breakfast appointment." And I've stayed with it. Exercising has become a religion for me.

You have to make a decision that this one thing is more important than something else. My whole life could be eaten up literally and figuratively by breakfast appointments and lunch appointments and dinner appointments. It's easy to blow off exercise, so what I find is if I do it very early in the morning, it's over and done with.

There's no question when you get into your 40s and 50s, your body changes even though you might not have put on any weight. My weight is probably eight pounds different than when I was 22, but your body is different. And you feel that. You see it and you feel it. Again, I think exercise doesn't always help you lose weight, but it can help you realign the parts of your body that are bothering you.

A few years ago at a conference called Mind, Body, and Soul, which I host for our female advertisers, we had Suze Orman, the financial guru, speak. She said to this group of 80 or 100 women, she just came out and said, "How many of you know exactly what's in your stock portfolio right now? How many know about your investments? How many give all the responsibility to some financial planner that you're paying a percentage to and you don't even know what the percentage is?" And every woman was like [makes a gesture to show they were bracing in their seats]. It was confronting something that maybe more women than men don't adapt to real comfortably. They were acknowledging that there isn't going to be anybody else in their life to contribute. Or that maybe they just don't like dealing with all that financial stuff. So I think that in addition to your health and fitness regime, I think it's very good advice to really get on top of your finances early on. The younger, the better.

We are obviously a country that fears looking old. Yet, exercising is one of the only proven ways to stay young. It's right under our nose. Exercising is not just about developing a toned body and losing weight. It's about keeping your body as young as possible. You *can* keep yourself as fit at 65 as you were at 40. You can, at 80, have as healthy a heart as someone 20 years younger! In Part III, "Your Soul," Zig Ziglar, the highly popular and successful motivational speaker, remarks that he can stay longer on the treadmill at well into his 70s than when he was 45, overweight, and out of shape.

The problem is the power of exercise is often recognized only when it is too late, usually when you have been hit with an injury or disability (such as arthritis) that limits your mobility. Or after you develop a disease, such as diabetes. It's never too late to start exercising, but at the same time, don't wait until it's a lot harder for you to do it. Better to start at an optimal point than when you are hurting already.

Perhaps the reason why we are so obsessed with our aging appearance is because that's all we can see. We can see the wrinkles, the thinning hair, the age spots. However, we can't see exactly what's going on underneath the skin. Out of sight, out of mind.

The truth is, the signs of aging are apparent just after your 18th birthday, *before* the wrinkles and the balding begin. Starting at 20, your maximum breathing—which helps measure your physical fitness—starts to decline. Muscle mass starts to decrease after 30. After age 35, bone mineral loss begins to outpace bone mineral replacement. From age 20 to 80, your cardiac output—the amount of blood pumped in a minute—falls about 30 percent, owing to a decline in your maximum heart rate.

Exercising is the one *easy* thing you can do to counter these processes. Exercise slows the loss of muscle mass. It helps prevent rapid loss of bone minerals. In some studies, researchers found that older adult athletes who exercised regularly were as physically fit as those in their middle ages. In other words, if you exercise every day, you keep your heart, and all systems related to your cardiovascular health, *younger* than everybody else's at your age. Can you imagine if you could do something every day to keep your face looking younger than your friends? You would jump at this! This is the same thing, only the results are inside your body. Improving your heart is more important to aging well than getting rid of a few wrinkles.

Some types of exercises help in specific ways. Michael Irwin, a doctor who runs the Cousins Center for Psychoneuro-immunology at UCLA, found that older patients who attended regular Tai Chi Chih classes became less susceptible to shingles, a disease that commonly afflicts the elderly. He found it helped increase the cell-mediated immunity (an immune response that does not involve the usual antibodies) to the varicella zoster virus, which causes shingles, by as much as 50 percent one week after the 15-week class session finished. Dr. Irwin compared the physical improvement to having hip replacement surgery or heart valve replacement. It was *that* significant.

"We only looked at shingles immunity, but there's no reason to believe that this can't extend to other viral infections," he told us.

Researchers are just beginning to discover the benefits of exercise on aging processes they long thought were inevitable. Take arteriosclerosis (the hardening of your arteries): People used to believe that this stiffening was a natural, if still unwanted, part of aging. The stiffening causes high blood pressure, which can lead to stroke, coronary artery disease, heart attack, and heart failure—some of the worst conditions to hit people older than 50. Think how much harder your heart has to pump to get blood through these stiff arteries.

Recent studies have found that people who regularly engage in endurance exercises, such as running on a treadmill, have less hardening of the arteries than those in the same group who didn't exercise. Other studies found that people who could walk the longest on a treadmill—meaning they were the most physically fit—also had the most pliable arteries. As a heart report issued by the National Institute on Aging states, "Endurance training may give us at least some control over the condition of the arteries— a process we thought *controlled us* [our emphasis]."

However, let's not rely on data alone to motivate us to exercise. It doesn't matter how many studies you read, it's still pretty darn hard to get up and move when you want to lay around and eat potato chips. Or work on that special sales report. Or do whatever else that prevents you from stepping on a treadmill.

The government advises us to exercise at least five days a week for 30 minutes at a time. Private health trainers either adhere to this frequency or suggest alternatives. Some say you can exercise three or four times a week for an hour and others say you can slice up your exercise regime in 10- or 15-minute segments throughout the day, every day.

That's the problem. When you have too many options to fit exercise into your routine, the undesirable result happens—you tend to regard exercise itself as an option. It's something you "fit" into your schedule whenever you can. For all the good intentions of flexible scheduling, exercise loses its urgency when it's regarded as something that can be sliced, diced, and quartered into our daily routines.

You have to look at exercise the same as other job or family commitments. We agree with Cathie Black. If you have to, schedule it into your Palm Pilot or desk calendar. Schedule your commitments *around* exercise; tell friends you have a pressing appointment and just close yourself off for 30 minutes. Do it for at least 30 minutes straight and get it over with. Don't bother with 5-, 10-, or 15-minute segments—why clutter up your mind with even more things to keep track of? And don't cheat. You did an hour one day, so you think you can do 15 minutes the next. Sorry, no dice. You need at least a half hour to get your heart rate up and benefit from any type of endurance exercise, whether it be jogging, swimming, or mopping the floor. Thirty minutes, in the grand view of your day, is *nothing*. If the average American can spend four hours in front of the tube, he or she can surely carve out 30 minutes (even adding in the time it takes to travel back and forth from the gym)!

Get some form of exercise every day, Saturdays and Sundays included. There's no such thing as "weekend breaks" when it comes to exercise. Exercise *every single day* for the rest of your life. That's non-negotiable. The only time you might take a day off in between for breaks is if you're doing some heavy-duty weight lifting, but then that just means taking a break *from weight lifting*—not from exercising. You wouldn't try to stop eating every day, right? Exercise is as crucial to your health and well-being as eating. So, our first rule of exercise is to get your heart pumping every day.

The second rule has to do with how to make this everyday commitment more palatable. You can do this by varying your exercise routine. You don't have to spend every day at the gym. That can get pretty boring after a while. How many of us have joined a gym and revved up to test out the new equipment and saunas and other perks, only to lose interest after three or four weeks? Then, we feel guilty about buying that annual membership and not using it, which then prevents us from taking a class at the local yoga studio or buying at-home exercise equipment.

Dr. Richard Steadman: "Surgeon to the Stars"

After interviewing numerous successful people in this book, we quickly noticed a pattern. A number of them were physically active throughout their lives. It was absolutely crucial in helping them age well. Another common factor was a man named Dr. Richard Steadman. Whenever someone told us of an injury or a joint problem, they often mentioned they went to see this doctor. We had to find out why.

Dr. Steadman is arguably one of the world's best orthopedic surgeons, having helped pioneer cutting-edge treatments for joint problems that are now used throughout the world. For example, Dr. Steadman was among the first physicians to encourage patients to exercise shortly after joint surgery to speed up recovery rather than continue the usual practice of remaining immobile. He practices on the best (and most vulnerable) bones and joints in the world—from Olympic skiers to NBA basketball players.

More than a "surgeon to the stars," Dr. Steadman runs the Steadman-Hawkins Clinic (www.Steadman-hawkins.com) in Vail, Colorado. The clinic treats both regular folks and sports superstars for their injuries and, through

Dr. Steadman's foundation, conducts research into the latest techniques and treatments for joint disorders. He's the chief physician for the U.S. Olympic Ski Team and a longtime athlete, having played football for Bear Bryant at Texas A&M University. ("The Bear," of course, became a living legend coaching there and at the University of Alabama.) At age 68, Dr. Steadman regularly hits the slopes just outside his office. If you have a problem with your joints, he's the man.

One of the things we *don't* want you to do after reading this book is to start running three miles on a treadmill. Why? Because you're going to kill your joints. We have a tendency to feel so guilty about not exercising that we go overboard and start off in one big huff. What happens then? We guarantee the day after you will feel as if you swam the English Channel. But worse than that, you might hurt yourself.

As Dr. Steadman explained to us, your joints are equipped with shock absorbers. Muscles are positioned around your joints to protect them like big, soft pillows. If you haven't exercised in a while, the muscles are most likely going to be weak. They won't be able to handle the shock of you suddenly pounding on them for a half hour as you try to run your "I-haven't-done-this-in-five-years" marathon.

"I think some people—and I've seen it happen—say, 'It's time. I've done nothing for 20 years, I'm gonna get in shape,'" Dr. Steadman said. "And instead of doing it in a gradual way, which doesn't put a lot of strain on the joints before the muscles are prepared to protect them from strain, they crank the resistance up to a max and go for 30 minutes and then they feel so bad that they can't exercise for a long length of time."

So what is Dr. Steadman's advice? Take it slow when you start out again. Have mini-goals that don't require a lot of strain. You will also feel better and more accomplished. That's what Dr. Steadman tells his patients, some of whom are the world's best athletes. Imagine telling sports stars, such as Olympic skiers Picabo Street and Bode Miller, to take it slow after they've been laid up with an injury! They are raring to go—no time until the next competition. However, as Dr. Steadman explained further, starting slowly makes the most sense.

I've probably had over 20 people who have won Olympic medals after their treatment [with me]. I think the thing that was universal in each of their cases was that they had the ability to focus on the goal. And, in their case, the long-term goal was to be back skiing and effectively participating and winning medals. But to get to that goal, they had to focus on short-term goals.

Let's say that a great skier has had a major injury. They can't wake up every morning thinking about standing on the podium at the Olympics. They've got to think about identifying a short-term goal, such as being able to get a full range of motion after the surgery, and that should be something that they get a psychological reward for if they are able to achieve this goal. Then, the next goal might be to ride a stationary bike for a relatively short period of time and then increasing lengths of time. And that should be the next goal in therapy. And then that just feeds on itself. In other words, as you reach one short-term goal, then you go to the next short-term goal.

If I had a message to get out to people, it is that sometimes you have to change your goals as you go from being 20 to 30 to 60 to 70 in exercise. But you don't have to stop exercising. And I think it's equally as important for me today, at 68, to exercise—I'm on my way right now actually—to be able to have an active life and to have an active, productive business life.

I think there are two types of exercise. One is based on overload and that would be a weight[-lifting] program. You need a day of recuperation from that type of exercise. If you're doing something that's not overload but repetitive load, such as a stationary bike or walking or hiking, something like that, generally, you can do that every day. I would take a day off when you feel fatigued, but if you don't feel fatigued, then it's not necessary to take a day off just for muscle recuperation.

I believe in identifying exercise—or parts of exercises—that match with any physical problems that you might have. For example, it's very common in people with advancing age, even for people over 40, to develop problems in the kneecap and the area where the kneecap rubs. So, if you have developed that kind of problem as you progress toward age 40 plus, then there are exercises that you can do that maintain your physical sense of well-being, but put less pressure on the problem area. So, I think it's helpful to recognize a problem area and then set up your exercise program around that problem area.

For example, we've done research here that would say that if you have a kneecap problem, that if you do mild to moderate uphill walking, that's probably your best exercise. And I think it's counterintuitive in a way to people because if you do general uphill walking, then it puts less pressure on the patella [knee cap]. On the other hand, if you walk upstairs, you bend your knee more and that puts more pressure on it. And if you walk downstairs or downhill, that puts increased pressure on. So, identifying the things that work best for you would be the best way to avoid problems, number one—and allow you to continue, number two.

One of the easy things to do as a first step in getting back in shape would be to ride a stationary bike. And if you start out on a stationary bike, you should start out with facing no resistance and a moderate length of time on the bike. You can actually create damage if you try to do too much resistance early. I think it's important to start gradually if you're trying to get into an exercise program and allow the muscles to gain a level of strength and ability to be protective before amplifying on the exercise program.

The body is an amazing machine, but the place people get off track is when they try to do too much exercise too soon.

So take the doctor's advice. Hundreds of famous athletes and superstars have. Start out slow and small. Work your way up. But whatever you do, **don't stop**.

So, our second rule is this: Keep your time commitment, but change your exercise routine. Routine is good for you, but if it gets too dull, it can wreak havoc on your exercise habits. Exercise has greatly diversified over the last several decades, giving you several options from which to choose. Yoga studios are opening up around the country. Older people have come to love Tai Chi Chih—the westernized version of the Chinese martial art, Tai Chi Chuan. Pilates, a German import, is another popular regime. Dr. Irwin said in his study of Tai Chi Chih, the attendance rate was quite high, probably because the martial arts class was novel, interesting, and social. In other studies, using traditional exercise techniques, such as walking, Dr. Irwin professed that many of his patients stopped attending and some were hiding or running away from his researchers when they were looking for them!

If you get bored going to one studio, join another one after the session ends. If you are tired of going out all the time to exercise, buy a workout video and spend time at home. Join a gym if you want but try to keep the fees month-to-month—that way, you won't feel guilty if you decide to spend money on something else.

Don't think of exercise as something you do only in tights or shorts. Sign up for horseback riding lessons. Or learn how to ski during the winter months. Garden. Swim. Vacuum. Whatever you do, keep in mind you want to get at least these four things out of it:

- Endurance training (increases stamina, exercises your heart)
- Strength training (builds up muscle mass)
- Stretching (keeps you flexible)
- Balance (keeps you steady on your feet and prevents falls and accidents)

Most exercise regimes do all four, so don't fret about this too much; however, if you choose only to garden, try running up and down the stairs for a few minutes afterward to build up your strength and endurance. Before you swim, try stretching. Don't get too bogged down in details. We don't want you to start worrying about whether you've gotten enough strength training today or stretching yesterday. Just exercise! You'll be way ahead of the curve.

You might find that after a while, you like sticking to one exercise regime. Stay with it. You've reached nirvana. The important thing now is not to fall off the wagon. Research shows that if you stop exercising after just two weeks, the benefits of exercise start to wear off. After two to eight months, the benefits disappear *altogether*. It's like starting from scratch again—don't let that happen to you.

For many people, the first month is the hardest. If you haven't exercised in months, or years, you'll find it tough to stay committed the first month. After 30 days, reward yourself with something—a slice of chocolate cake, a massage, a new dress, or an electronic gadget. You'll feel terrific.

Also, don't forget to log your exercise habits. We take a page out of the government playbook on this. The Department of Health and Human Services suggests you keep data on your activities every day so you can track your progress. The more detailed, the better, but generally, something like, "30 minutes, walked 2 miles" is good. Writing your exercise routine down is a great way to stay organized and to reinforce the idea that this is a commitment. A job. A daily task.

Every month, test yourself to see if you're actually improving. The reward is knowing you are not only enhancing the way you look and how you feel but also actually ensuring that you stay younger *longer*. Later on, we tell you about other benefits of exercise, such as helping keep your brain healthy and boosting your mood.

For now, remember that exercise will do wonders for your age. It's one true secret to the fountain of youth. Isn't that motivation enough?

Exercise Worksheet

Target Heart Rates During Endurance Exercise

For a person in their

40s	126-153
50s	119-145
60s	112-136
70s	105-128
80s	98-119
90s	91-111
100s	84-102 (hooray for you!)

Source: National Institute on Aging

Ways to Measure Your Progress
Check each on the first of each month:

	Jan.	Feb.	Mar.	Apr.	May	Jun.	July	Aug.	Sept.	Oct.	Nov.	Dec.
Endurance: Measure how far you're able to walk in six minutes.												
Lower Body Strength: Time how fast you can walk up a flight of stairs—at least 10 steps.												
Balance: Time yourself as you stand on one foot, and then the other, without support.												

Source: National Institute on Aging

Kenneth Cooper: "Father of Aerobics"

Before there was yoga, Pilates, and Billy Blanks' Tae Bo, there was plain and simple aerobics. Get your legwarmers and tights or shorts on and hit the gym floor to some disco music. Aerobics was *the* way to get your heart pumping and your rear end smaller.

Exercise has changed through the years, but the person who many call the "father of aerobics" is still encouraging millions of people to get fit to stay healthy. From a simple book titled *Aerobics* in 1968, Dr. Kenneth Cooper helped introduce the concept of prevention through exercise to millions of Americans and thus boosted, unbeknownst to him, a multi-billion-dollar fitness industry (and a second career for Jane Fonda).

At 75, Dr. Kenneth Cooper is busier than ever running his Cooper Aerobics Center in Dallas, Texas, which includes a clinic, a research center, a spa, and, of course, a state-of-the-art fitness center. He has written dozens of books, has several in the works, and hosts radio and television shows. His clinic sees more than 90,000 patients with a message that has remained the same over three decades: *prevention* is the best medicine.

We were surprised to discover how spiritual Dr. Cooper is. Before becoming a physician, Dr. Cooper had thought about joining the missionary. He attributes his incredible success to "divine intervention" and knows full well the value of family and its role in helping him live a healthy life. Even for Dr. Cooper, a long life consists of more than just exercising and eating right—it includes keeping your soul happy and your social network full, topics we talk about in Part III, "Your Soul."

Although aerobics was popularized as an efficient way to tone and trim the body, Dr. Cooper's focus is in using exercise to slow aging. He works with thousands of older patients to see how consistent exercise might even *reverse* the aging process.

We used to teach in medical schools that after 60 years of age, you can't build up new muscle mass. After 60 years of age, you can't improve your cardiovascular conditioning. Well, those [beliefs] are totally in error because we're finding that, as we grow older, our bodies deteriorate, not so much because we're growing old, but because we're constantly doing less physically as we grow old.

In other words, we're rusting up, not wearing out. I have some classic examples of older people who are just rewriting the textbooks. One of my favorite friends is Fan Benno. She's kind of legendary around our center here. She's 87 years of age and still competes internationally in walking events. Recently, she set a world record for a woman over 85 years of age in walking 3,000 meters. This summer, she's participating in the senior Texas event—Ms. Senior Texas. That's for women over 60 years of age. She made this wonderful statement in a letter to me. She told me, "Dr. Cooper, because of you, I forgot to grow old." What a marvelous statement.

A study was done and a book written by Miriam Nelson entitled Strong Women, Strong Bones. *She followed a group of 40 women through 50 weeks. These women were on average about 61 years of age, all post-menopausal for at least five years.*

During the next 50 weeks, half of them did nothing but take 80 milligrams of calcium daily. The other half took 80 milligrams of calcium daily and worked out 45 minutes twice a week. She looked at bone density measurements and did strength measurements. At the end of 50 weeks, [Nelson] found that those women, even though they took no hormone replacement therapy, even though their average age was 61 years old, those women who took the calcium and exercised twice a week had the highest percentage increase of their bone density in their back and their hips and increased their muscle mass. The control group who didn't exercise but took the calcium—they all lost strength and lost muscle mass and bone mass during that period of time, proving contrary to what we thought before that you can't build up muscle mass in post-menopausal women after 60 years of age.

I've had women who've actually increased their height after they get involved in an exercise rehab program. We actually have an 83-year-old woman who has increased her height about a half an inch since she started and went into our program.

I have tried to take care of myself both spiritually and physically. And when I combine those two every day, it makes what I've called an A day. I classify my productivity daily as being A, B, or C.

And some days, everything works correctly. I rip through my patients, I have great responses, I'm not wasting any time whatsoever, and I call that an A day. Other days, it just doesn't work. I get interrupted with telephone calls. I can't start to do something, I can't get anything done. And I call those C days. So, I shoot for B days, at least.

If I start my day with my creative prayer and meditation, it almost always makes it an A day.

I hope that what I'll be able to do is square off the curve—that is, living a long and healthy life, living it to the fullest, and then dying suddenly. That's squaring off the curve. Stay near your peak, then drop suddenly near the end, rather than experience a steady decline over many years. Compress the time of morbidity and mortality into a short period immediately prior to death.

My parents succeeded in squaring off the curve. My father was a practicing dentist. He worked all day on Saturday and died on Monday and he was 77. He squared off the curve. My mother voted in the presidential election back in 1984. She went home that night to watch the election returns on the television. We found her [passed away] the next morning, living in her own home by herself, with the television still on. She was 82 years of age. She was driving her own car, totally independent, and I can assure you what she feared worse than death was losing her independence. Both my mother and father squared off the curve.

It's interesting that aerobics has stood the test of time over the past 37 years because it's basic and everybody knows that walking, running, cycling, and swimming are good for you. If you just go out and walk for 30 minutes, three times a week, and cover two miles during that time, you can reduce death by all causes by 58 percent and increase your life span by six years.

I've found over the years that [exercise fads] come and go. Jane Fonda came out in 1975 with aerobics being interpreted as aerobic dancing. Aerobic dancing is only one of some 41 different exercises that qualify as being aerobic. Then there came low-impact aerobics. And then step aerobics. There's been this slow progression of these various exercises because people burn out. They want new types of activities or they got hurt with the last activity.

Walking, running, cycling, swimming—those still form the basis of any good conditioning program. All these other things are add-ons.

Another powerful argument from one of the world's best doctors to encourage you to exercise. Dr. Cooper's view has always been that exercise doesn't have to be overly complicated. If you just get up and walk around the block a few times, you are going to live years longer. Who can resist the simplicity in that?

CHAPTER

3

Eat the Right Stuff

Every year, about 50 million—*50 million*—Americans go on a diet. Yet, the inevitable almost always happens—95 percent gain all the weight back. If everyone in this country had to put a dollar into a national account for every pound they gained back on a diet, we probably wouldn't be worrying about the future bankruptcy of Social Security and Medicare anymore!

Diets, by function of their design, will never work. They promise immediate results without the long-term lifestyle changes. It's like taking a Tylenol to ease knee pain. You'll feel better in the short-term, but unless you stop running and putting even more strain on those knee joints, you'll never get better. You will keep taking more Tylenol until it doesn't work that well anymore (and you ruin your joints).

Here's a secret. You'll lose weight if you eat fewer calories than you expend.

It's that simple.

Around the time we were writing this book, Morgan Spurlock came out with his controversial documentary, *Super Size Me*, which chronicled his one-month experiment eating nothing but McDonald's fast food. By now, you've probably heard about the results—how his cholesterol skyrocketed, how he became moody and sluggish, gained weight, and by the enormous publicity surrounding his film, eventually helped force McDonald's to eliminate its super-size program (though McDonald's has denied this and has since been offering healthier options, such as yogurt and fresh fruit).

Just think, it took a young man to sacrifice his health and produce a film to *state the obvious?* How can anyone think that eating fried, greasy foods for a month wouldn't cause serious health problems (though this seemed to exclude his clueless doctors)?

Diets are little experiments we do every year, or several times a year, to avoid the painfully obvious. Dr. C. Everett Koop, the former U.S. surgeon general, prescribed for us in his interview the only guaranteed way to lose weight. He boiled it down to a simple math equation: eat less calories than you burn. Calories and energy expended need to exceed calories ingested. The problem is that owning up to this math equation takes tremendous commitment and willpower, and, perhaps most problematic, it takes a *long* time. The South Beach Diet is popular because you can lose 10 pounds in two weeks. The same claim is also made by other diets, professional and amateur, from the Slim Fast diet to the "I'll eat cottage cheese for two weeks" diet.

The first thing you should do is stop dieting. That'll be probably one of the best gifts you can give your body. Imagine the strain you've placed on your body with all the ups and downs of rapid weight loss and gain.

This doesn't mean you should stop losing weight. If there's one surefire way to shorten your life—and make you age faster— it is obesity. An article in the *New England Journal of Medicine* stated that obesity can cut one-third to three-fourths of a year from a person's life, which sounds small until researchers point out the effect of obesity on life expectancy could soon become bigger than cancer or coronary artery disease (narrowing of the arteries that then restricts blood flow to the heart). Obesity itself might not be a major cause of death, but it certainly puts you at a much higher risk for all kinds of diseases—from coronary artery disease to diabetes to certain types of cancer—that *do* cut lives short.

Many of the people we have talked to who have aged well mentioned how little weight they've gained since their early twenties. A few were overweight at points in their lives, but when they made conscious efforts to be healthy again, they lost the extra pounds.

The Skinny on a Long Life

This entire book is about how there is not *one* secret to living longer; however, we have to admit there *might* be one.

As far as scientists can tell, calorie restriction might be the closest we come to slowing down aging. Reducing caloric intake has already extended the lives of yeast, worms, rats, and rhesus monkeys, sometimes by a staggering 40 percent. First tested in the 1930s by Dr. Clive McCay, calorie restriction is thought to reduce the incidence of diseases such as diabetes and even some cancers because, logically enough, many of these diseases are linked to obesity. Calorie restriction also alters oxidative damage, metabolism, and insulin sensitivity—all the processes and factors that can impact aging. This drives home the point that what you eat can *really* affect your entire aging process.

Why hasn't this caught on with droves of Americans wanting to stay young? Well, for one thing, real calorie restriction is extremely uncomfortable. You would have to eat 30 percent to 40 percent less, keeping you in a constant state of low-grade hunger. There's also the risk of mood swings, your appearance changing, and if you take it too far, becoming anorexic.

That doesn't mean there aren't people experimenting with calorie restriction. The Calorie Restriction Society, formally established in 2002, has a website (www.calorierestriction.org) that supports people practicing this diet. The National Institute on Aging has created CALERIE, which is short for Comprehensive Assessment of Long Term Effects of Reducing Intake of Energy and is conducting clinical trials on calorie restriction. It is unlikely most Americans will go for such an austere diet, but if scientists can decipher what's causing calorie reduction to slow the aging process and then bottle it in a pill, you bet that'll be a $100 billion discovery.

The goal is not to be super skinny, of course, but to be trim. Most of us can't be at the weight we were when we were 18—but as long as you keep your Body Mass Index (BMI) below thresholds, you are doing fine. (The National Heart Lung and Blood Institute has an easy BMI calculator at www.nhlbisupport.com/bmi/.) A BMI more than 30 is considered obese, by the way.

The key is to lose this weight slowly and naturally by eating fewer calories than you burn. Nutritiondata.com is a great website that details the calories of most common foods. If you can, splurge on a scale (they cost between $30 to $200) that weighs and calculates the number of calories on a variety of foods. If an average American man burns 2,500 calories per day and a woman 2,000 calories, then just consume, say, 10 percent less than that on a daily basis. (For a more accurate picture of how many calories you burn on average, go to About.com and type in "calorie per day calculator" in the search box on the upper right corner.) The best part is if you are active and exercising, as we asked you to do in the previous chapter, you get to eat a little more. (www.caloriesperhour.com tells you how many calories you burn with various types of exercising, from housework to jogging.)

If you are reading this and you *are* obese, this might not work for you. At this point, your weight problem is not about a little extra flab but about your health. If you are in the category of obese, we would suggest you consult with your doctor about ways to lose the weight safely, because a slow weight loss program might not be good enough for you. You might need to shed those pounds fast. The important thing for you is to read our recommendations on how to eat right. After you lose the weight, it's *critical* you keep it off.

Our first rule for better eating is *everything in moderation*. This is a good rule of thumb when you face anything you think is sinful. Everything you consume is okay as long as you don't go overboard. There are good and bad things about salt, good and bad things about sugar, good and bad things about fat, and good and bad things about caffeine. You get the picture.

You have probably read a study about a food being good for you only to read later that it might also be bad. Women are often faced with confusing information about what types of fish, an excellent source of protein, are safe to eat while pregnant because of concerns about mercury levels.

Sometimes, the opposite happens. Avocadoes were once forbidden because they were so fatty but now are devoured in guacamole dips everywhere because research revealed the fats were the "good" fats—helping lower cholesterol. We were once told to avoid alcohol at all costs, only to hear later that red wine *in moderation* can help your longevity by protecting against certain cancers and lowering your blood pressure and cholesterol. Studies show moderate drinking can help make you smarter, which might be why writers always have a few bottles stowed away in their cabinets.

There are few things that defy this moderation rule in life— smoking is one example. Don't do it! Generally speaking, you can sneak in those gummy bears or fried chicken drumsticks or ice cream sundaes as long as you don't eat them *every single day.*

In a 2002 survey from the American Dietetic Association, the latest one available, one poll showed that Americans were getting smarter about what to put in their bodies—38 percent of us were eating much healthier in 2002 compared to 26 percent in 1997. Some nutritionists cautiously say eating trends now tend to be the best in years, emphasizing whole grains, fish, good oils such as olive and canola, and lean meats. Yet disturbingly, our obesity rates are still climbing. Why is this?

A large part of this has to do not only with what we eat but also *how much of it.* Portion size is way out of control. We have a good chuckle whenever someone mentions how "small" soda cups are overseas, as if the 7-Eleven Super Gulp is the most natural amount anyone should consume in a sitting period.

The government has not helped—in fact, they have probably made it worse. For the longest time, the Food and Drug Administration told us to eat x-number of "servings" of vegetables, pastas, and fruits without making it easy for us to figure out what exactly a single serving was. Each serving for each category of food was different—for leafy vegetables, a half cup; for meats, a deck of cards; and so on. Who in this world cooks and eats by servings?

Then we ate at restaurants, where portion sizes got larger and larger through the 1980s, 1990s, and 2000s. Food is cheap in

America, so restaurants can afford to heap a box of pasta on your plate and charge you less than ten bucks. It makes you feel like you are getting more bang for your buck.

Dr. Louis W. Sullivan: A Pioneer In Medical Education

This book would be incomplete without discussing the fact that, despite our advances in longevity research and the reality that many Americans are living into their 80s, 90s, and beyond in good shape, for a substantial portion of people in this country, life expectancy is not where it should be.

The advances in medicine have not always been available to poor people, particularly in minority groups and rural areas. Many African-Americans living in several parts of the country either cannot afford quality medical care or even get access to it. Basic health education is still limited in some of the poorest parts of the country. To people living paycheck to paycheck, financial advice about "managing a portfolio" sounds ridiculous. The poorest parts of the U.S. have the highest infant mortality rates and shortest life expectancies (see Appendix, "The Baby Boomer Factor and Life Expectancy," for more analysis).

These concerns are reasons why the work of Dr. Louis W. Sullivan has been so important. As founding president of the Morehouse School of Medicine in Atlanta and former Secretary of The U.S. Department of Health and Human Services, Dr. Sullivan has made it his mission to expand healthcare and medical services to the most underserved communities in the U.S. He grasped the need for more African-American physicians and more primary care doctors and is trying to fulfill this goal through his pioneering work at Morehouse.

Dr. Sullivan graduated from Morehouse before carving an illustrious medical career that culminated in his appointment as Health Secretary by President George H.W. Bush in 1989.

We wanted to speak with 72-year-old Dr. Sullivan for his sage advice on eating well and exercising and to find out some of the universal truths he believes will help everyone live a healthy and happy life. The following is what he had to say:

I certainly do not subscribe to retiring at 65. First of all, we as a society and as individuals are living significantly longer. And not only living longer, but the quality of those years is also better. Those who do not remain active often decline, both in terms of their interests in things and being interesting people, as well as their physical health. I believe that people who are actively engaged in things that they enjoy doing and that capture their imagination—whether it is working for money or volunteer work—really remain dynamic and remain healthy for a longer period of time. To me, there's no question that this has a very definite physical and mental benefit for the individual. In my view, having a really challenging activity, whether it is work or volunteering or a hobby, has definite benefits because it becomes an organizing principle for that person's life.

I would say, thinking of my own career, that people do age better mentally and physically when they find new activities or hobbies to stretch themselves. The fact is I became Emeritus at Morehouse Medical School three years ago, and although I'm still active in doing some things for the medical school, I've become active in working to develop a National Health Museum in Washington. This is a volunteer activity now, but I gain intellectually because I have found it to be a very challenging goal. In fact, I tell my friends, I finally found something that's harder than raising money—that's getting land in Washington, near the Washington Mall! The concept of the museum is really to improve the health literacy of Americans. And through that, to improve the health behavior of our citizens, which will have an impact on improving their health status and in the long term, reducing healthcare costs.

The genesis for the founding of the Morehouse School of Medicine was an ambition, starting in the mid-50s, to increase the number of physicians in the U.S. because it was feared that we would be facing a doctor shortage if we could not expand medical education in this country. After all, the Baby Boomer generation was swelling the population that would need doctors. Morehouse School of Medicine was one of the 46 new medical schools that came into being. We were clearly needed because at the time the concept of developing a medical school at Morehouse arose, during the early 1970s, only two percent of the physicians in the United States were African-American. Morehouse was unique—the one new medical school that was predominantly African-American.

The school's mission, in addition to training more minority physicians, was to orient our students toward careers as primary care physicians, for example, in family medicine, general internal medicine, or general pediatrics. We succeeded because we consistently rank at or very close to the top of all medical schools in the percentage of our graduates going into a primary care career, with roughly two-thirds in such areas.

In September of 2006, my wife and I celebrate our 50th anniversary. I know that for us, and I suspect this is also true for similar people with long marriages, we continue to be renewed, refreshed, and really enhanced by our relationship. Our children are all grown, and we're now able to do some things that we were not able to do when we had children in the house and had other financial obligations. I know for me and my wife, we find that these years are ones that are very exciting, very interesting. Surely for us, a long marriage has been very fulfilling and rewarding.

I think there is validity in the studies showing that married men live significantly longer than single men. Clearly, there are emotional and spiritual benefits from a relationship that has both psychological and physical benefits. This is similar to the finding that when a spouse is lost, the surviving spouse is at much greater risk of dying within a short period of time. I'm sure the converse of that, having a relationship that is rewarding and fulfilling and satisfying, has a very definite physical benefit that we see with individuals surviving longer and in better health.

You mention that the life expectancy for African-Americans is rising, and the gap with others is closing, but there is still a worrying gap. You ask what can African-Americans do to live longer, healthier lives? Well, let me comment on that.

First of all, one of the things that I do that I certainly recommend for everyone is to have a regular program of physical activity and physical exercise. I actually walk three miles every morning. Indeed, I walk about five miles on Saturday and Sunday. The key is to make it a habit; I miss that maybe a dozen days out of the year at most. And that will usually be a day when I have a six o'clock flight out of the airport or have to get up at four o'clock in the morning. But I've been doing that now for 30 years, and I find that this helps me a lot. Plus, it not only helps keep me fit and healthy but also helps me clear my head for the day. I find that if I can't walk for whatever reason, those are the days that by mid-afternoon, I'm often not as focused as I ordinarily am.

But, in addition to exercise, there are things that I think people can do and should do to try and protect their health. The key is having a balanced, proper diet. One of the problems we have now, of course, is obesity, from people having excess calories and an imbalanced diet. Clearly, I think people should avoid tobacco because that has nothing but negative consequences for your health.

Next, we need to obtain adequate rest. People who really burn the candle at both ends are at risk, as sooner or later that catches up with you. Your ability to function effectively is diminished as a result of too little sleep.

I see my doctor, my dentist, and my ophthalmologist at least once a year. I take multivitamins to be sure that I have a balanced intake of essential vitamins and minerals. All these things are important, especially after 50, because we are mortal bodies.

Also, take time off for reflection and for mental relaxation, because we, in our society now, are faced with a constant barrage of things going on all the time. It's important to have some quiet time to really collect and restore your mind and your body.

Rather than a particular diet program, I emphasize more general principles. In other words, I don't utilize these Dr. X Diets or what have you. By proper diet, I mean, for example, having a balanced intake of fruits, vegetables, lean meats, and seafood. Also, have an appropriate caloric intake. The average or normal caloric intake for a grown individual is really approximately 2,000 calories for women or men on the small side, maybe 2,200 calories for larger individuals. Too many of our diets really have 3,000, 3,500, even 4,000 calories—and that's certainly an excess. The balance really is crucial. For example, add fresh fruits and vegetables and among those, have a very wide variety of richly colored ones, not only green but yellow, red, and orange and various berry colors.

It is important to keep reading. Reading about nature and science and technology can keep your mind young, and it is so stimulating. I recommend the National Geographic Magazine. Each month, we can be transported to distant lands or space and learn about diverse cultures or species. Also, do not be afraid of the main science magazines and nature ones, as they can open new horizons for you.

Here is my concluding thought on aging smart. The key is to focus on a really challenging goal, one that takes real effort, such as sustained mental exertion. You gain the most when you are focused and truly challenged. I have a guiding principle, to have goals that take real effort to achieve.

Our rule of moderation absolutely applies to how much you eat, too. The amount Americans eat is *not normal*. It's too much. We are just too used to it. Always opt for the half size plates at a restaurant. Or immediately bag half your plate of food at the start of the meal. If it's not there in front of you, you won't eat it. Avoid the all-you-can-eat buffets—just the concept is opposed to our moderation rule! Resist the urge to eat seconds of anything. Drink small everything or better yet, just drink water. No super-sizing anything, but wait, that's already been taken care of for you by Morgan Spurlock.

Our second rule is to *get naked*. Study after study makes the case that people who stick to naked foods tend to have populations with lower incidences of heart disease and more people living to older ages. By naked, we mean whole foods— not processed. You know, like a tomato. Or some blueberries. A grilled chicken breast. Things a four-year-old could name.

There are large populations of people who eat naked foods and live longer, healthier lives. The Okinawan diet (see the books by Wilcox, Wilcox, and Suzuki laying out *The Okinawa Program*), famous because the Japanese island is home to an unusually large number of centenarians, emphasizes fish, whole grains, and fresh vegetables. Scientists recently proclaimed the Mediterranean diet, rich in olive oils, tomatoes, fish, cheese, another recipe for a longer life.

The case of the Pima Indians is another example. About 200 years ago, white settlers disrupted the Pima Indians' traditional way of life in America, forcing them onto reservations in Arizona where they were first introduced to Western staples, such as white starch and sugar, otherwise known as refined foods. It wasn't until after World War II that the Pimas truly began to eat a Western diet filled with high fat, high sugar, and processed ingredients. The result: the Pimas in Arizona developed one of the worst cases of diabetes and heart disease among a specific group of people. A large number grew morbidly obese. Nearly one half of the Pima adults were diagnosed with diabetes. The more sedentary lifestyles of the Arizona Pimas didn't help either—something else they adopted from our culture.

But the kicker? A genetically similar group of Pimas who settled in rural Mexico and maintained their typical diet of corn, grains, and lean meats have stayed mostly diabetes-free. That's right; by sticking to a diet of more naked ingredients and avoiding processed foods, despite having similar genetic backgrounds, the Mexican Pima Indians avoided the debilitating diseases afflicting their brethren in Arizona. Remember what we said at the beginning about genes playing only a 20 percent to 30 percent role in our longevity? This is proof!

You should be able to tell what is in your food by just looking at it—totally undressed in front of you. Keep foods from jars, cans, boxes, and styrofoam to a minimum every day. The problem with many processed foods—from ranch dressing to Stouffers Chicken Pot Pie—is that there are loads of salt, sugar, additives, and other things that you simply do not need. We know it won't be easy to do this. Fast food is fast food— it's convenient, easy, and probably works best on the days you are swamped at work or at home with the children (and we are not just talking about the stuff coming out of the drive-thru—there's plenty of fast food at the supermarket). Do your best to get the grilled instead of the fried; the water instead of the sugared drink; the fresh fruit instead of the apple pie. Remember that everything is okay, as long as you do it in moderation.

On the other hand, the fact that many more Americans are becoming increasingly sophisticated about eating healthy means that there are an ever increasing variety of options to cater to your naked food needs. Salad bars—real scrumptious, not just lettuce leaves and tomatoes salad bars—are everywhere (only olive oil and vinegar please). You can get sandwiches on whole wheat bread. You can buy sushi—sushi!—at the local supermarket. (We can't attest to the flavor or style, though.) Organic produce is everywhere. Now's the best time to get naked!

Try your best to make every meal as naked as possible. Skip the decadent desserts for now or limit it to once a week (our moderation rule again). Get the dressings on the side. Cook at home as much as you can. Opt for steamed vegetables. If you just absolutely have to have that Big Mac fix, just make sure the next meal's a cleansing salad.

The next rule we recommend is to *watch the S foods: sugar, salt, and starches.* Every time you take a bite, a gazillion chemical reactions occur that researchers are only now beginning to understand. All those reactions are complicated even more by the fact that we have million-year-old biological systems in us dealing with a 21st century world of fast and processed food. Our bodies were not meant to process these kinds of foods. Some of the same processes that helped us survive the wilderness are absolutely killing us now.

The Pima Indians are a perfect example. Scientists puzzling over their marked rise in high blood pressure and diabetes attributed some of this to their genes, which have adapted to living conditions over thousands of years. Turns out, the Pimas were less able to deal with excess salt and sugar because their bodies had grown accustomed to being without after centuries of nomadic living, marked by periods of "feast and famine." Their bodies tended to hoard any excess food in extreme ways, preparing for that next tough period without food. Some scientists theorize they developed a "thrifty gene" to deal with such conditions. The result was that after the Pimas settled into a world of abundant food, their bodies couldn't reverse centuries of adaptation in a snap. Their bodies kept hoarding the food, producing rivers of insulin to process the glucose, storing the excess fat, waiting, their bodies thought, for the inevitable famine period. On their new diet, the Pimas got fat—and sick.

Some of this relates to the "revolutionary" diet trends we've heard of in the past few years, the so-called "low-carb" diets. By now, nutritionists concede the basic premise of the Atkins Diet, the South Beach Diet, and all those other low-carb successors is right: that simple carbs—what you find in starchy foods like white bread and pasta—are bad for you. They convert easily to glucose, cause spikes in your blood sugar, which then signal the production of more insulin, which lowers your blood sugar, making you feel even hungrier. No wonder our waistlines protrude by eating a loaf of French bread.

Protein has few carbohydrates and tends to keep your blood sugar levels stable, leaving you sated easier. That's why people on the Atkins Diet felt fuller and ate less food, thus losing weight (back to the less calories in, more calories out math equation again). The same goes with high-fiber foods, such as whole wheat bread or beans. The high-fiber content means it takes a lot longer for your body to convert these foods into glucose, which also leads to more stable blood sugar levels. Talk to any diabetic and they can tell you the "glycemic index" of lots of foods—for example, what a carrot stick does to your blood sugar level. (For more information, check out www.glycemicindex.com.)

Insulin and blood sugar are not things only diabetics should worry about. You can't eat French fries and donuts for the rest of your life and not put yourself at grave risk for diabetes, especially in your older years. Doctors are becoming much more sensitive to people who are *prediabetic*; they have a fasting blood sugar level between 100 to 125. Millions of people are *prediabetic* and don't even know it.

Sugar quickly turns into glucose. It immediately causes your blood sugar to rise and fall. Sugar itself is not an evil substance, despite the backlash it gets from the public. We need sugar for energy; however, we don't need *that* much of it. We consume 130 to 150 pounds of sugar a year, which means your insulin's probably ramping up to maximum levels just to process it all.

What happened to the Pima Indians happens to us, too. Diabetes is growing at an alarming rate—approximately 18.2 million Americans have the disease already. We eat French fries, processed foods with loads of sugar and starch, bread, pasta, potatoes—all those white foods—that wreak havoc on our blood sugar and insulin levels.

One basic lesson to learn from this low-carb craze—which we absolutely do not advocate because it's just another diet—is that it's *right* that you should watch your starches and sugars. The FDA has basically confirmed this with its revised nutritional pyramid. Keep an eye on carbohydrates in particular and apply the moderation rule. You shouldn't indefinitely avoid bread, pasta, fruits, and vegetables—that's ridiculous and dangerous. However, you can stop yourself from drinking high-fructose corn syrup in sodas and eating junk food. You can choose whole wheat or whole grain over refined grains. You can eat apples instead of ice cream.

Does the Rest of the World Get Fat?

We are sure you have heard this refrain once or twice before. How can the Italians eat all that pasta and not get so fat? Or how can the French indulge in all that wine and cheese and still stay so maddeningly skinny?

Sometimes, we look at Asian countries and see how their people can consume bowls upon bowls of white rice and nobody has any cellulite to show for it. What are they all doing right and what are we doing wrong?

Well, first of all, it all goes back to portion control. And exercise. Oh, and don't forget the moderation rule. It's all the habits we've talked about in these past two chapters. America is one of the greatest places to live, but it can be a hazard to your quest to stay fit and healthy. Things are just too convenient. You can literally get up in the morning, walk two paces to your SUV, drive through for a coffee and a sandwich, and arrive at work with nary a stain on your shoes. In China, people do eat lots of rice and noodles but remember that more than half the population work as laborers, meaning they tend the rice fields, build new skyscrapers, or transport goods. They are physically active.

And sometimes, things aren't always as they seem. There *are* overweight people in Italy, France, and China, though some people argue it's because now these countries have a plethora of American and domestic fast food chains.

One interesting thing we discovered is how the Chinese regard rice. In the U.S., we think nothing of gobbling rice with our Moo Shu pork, but in reality, many restaurants in China don't even give you the fluffy white stuff, unless you ask for it. It's regarded by the Chinese as a filler, the same way we view bread and pasta. A proper Chinese meal consists of delicious meat and vegetable dishes with only the rice added if you're still not satiated. We doubt the Atkins Diet has swept China, but it sure sounds like the Chinese know to limit the white starch.

So, do what the people in Europe and Asia do. Eat small portions. Keep to lean meats. Walk a lot. And throw out the dinner rolls—or at least save them for last.

The last "s" in this section has to do with salt. Salt puts you at risk for high blood pressure. Salt is also a necessary mineral for us. In huge quantities, though, it can turn ugly for you. Things you wouldn't think have abundant amounts of salt in them actually do, such as sweetened corn flakes. Store-bought breads have loads of salt.

Let's take a walk to our refrigerator, shall we? Let's see, oh here, a Schwebel's plain bagel, that should be obvious. Wow. Looks like it has 300 milligrams of sodium—13 percent of your necessary daily intake. Quite a lot for just one plain bagel. Let's try the cream cheese we would put on the bagel. Two tablespoons of Philadelphia Cream Cheese has 65 milligrams of sodium. A little better, but a lot of salt concentrated in such a small amount. How about something such as a can of sweetened condensed milk? Can't have salt in something that has the word "sweetened," right? Okay, only 40 milligrams of sodium, which sounds all right, but wait, that's for only one serving. There are supposedly 10 servings in this 14-ounce can, which means, whoa, that's *400 milligrams* of sodium, equal to about 17 percent of your necessary daily intake. You could consume more salt from downing a can of sweetened condensed milk than eating one bagel! Find the logic in that.

Make sure you read labels carefully (see how at the end of the chapter), and if you follow our naked rule, you'll likely not have to worry too much about your salt intake because you'll be in control of it.

Most of what we've told you is pure common sense. We will never go back to the diets we grew up on over thousands of years—roots, berries, and wild game—but we can certainly try to be as natural as possible and curb our tendency to overindulge.

We promise you will feel much better and you'll be doing your longevity a favor. Eating right is just one piece of this vast puzzle to aging well that we discuss in the rest of the book.

There are some people who can go through life eating nothing but fried chicken and smoking a pack a day and still live until 90. However, there are people who might have eaten only fish and vegetables, never smoked a day in their lives, and still get lung cancer. Like everything else we tell you in this book, aging is not about just Lady Luck. It's about taking control of the things you can control to give yourself a better chance at aging well. It's about playing the odds in your favor.

The Real Scoop on Food Labels

We don't advocate any specific diet plan or program, but we do agree with many of the healthy living advice and research coming out of the Pritikin Longevity Center & Spa in Aventura, Florida.

One particularly useful class they hold for visitors is on food labels. As if you didn't have enough to think about when it comes to healthy eating, food corporations make it more difficult for you by making food labels confusing and oftentimes, misleading. How low is low fat? A lot of times you would have to find out if the company is measuring the percentage of fat by weight or by the amount of calories. Is whole wheat really whole wheat? You would have to scrutinize the label for whole grain. How much salt do you consume in a serving of Frosted Flakes? Again, you would have to scour the labels for the fine print. Pritikin nutritionists even conduct their own experiments to verify the labels. In one case involving powdered cocoa, they found six out of eight popular brands were wrong in calculating the amount of fat in the cocoa!

Consumer advocate groups are starting to make these corporations more accountable for their food labels, forcing them to be more clear about what ingredients are in the foods they produce. Still, it can be a daunting edible jungle out there in your quest to eat smart.

As a courtesy, the Pritikin Center allowed us to reprint their ten tips for reading food labels, which we found to be extremely informative and user-friendly. These tips might not answer all your questions, but they are a good start. If you want to learn more, check out *Food Politics* by Marion Nestle or *Fast Food Nation* by Eric Schlosser. They are both fascinating reads about the dark side of the food industry.

Following are some basics of deciphering food labels, consolidated into 10 quick-reference tips, compliments of Jeffrey Novick, Director of Nutrition at the Pritikin Longevity Center & Spa.

1. **Never believe the claims on the front of the box.**

   What many think are health claims are actually just marketing pitches and advertisements. And government-approved claims, such as "low-fat" and "light," often don't tell you the whole story. These products might be high in fat as well as sugar, salt, and calories.

   "Light" ice cream, for example, might still pack in four to

five grams of fat per serving. And "light" and "regular" varieties of ice cream might not differ much calorically.

Never evaluate a product based on one item, such as its fat, cholesterol, sugar, carbohydrates, or salt content. Attempting to cash in on the latest diet or nutrition craze, many companies promote their products based on a single item despite other unhealthy aspects. (Remember "fat-free" foods that were full of sugar and calories?) To be truly healthy, a product must pass several criteria.

2. **Always read the Nutrition Facts label and the ingredient list.**

The label and the ingredient list contain information that can help you determine how healthy a food is. Crackers, for example, might advertise on the front of the box that they are "Trans Fat-Free," but in the ingredient list you might find fats, such as palm oil and coconut oil, that are just as artery-clogging as the trans fats they replaced.

3. **Check the serving size.**

Though the government standardized most serving sizes years ago, many products still post unrealistically small sizes. A serving of oil spray, for instance, is .25 grams. That's about 120th of an ounce—far less than most people could, or would, spray on a pan with even just one squirt.

4. **Check the amount of servings per package.**

Decades ago, many products were in fact single servings. A bottle of cola was one serving. One *small* candy bar was one serving. Today, many products are "super sized" and contain multiple servings. A 20-ounce bottle of soda contains 2.5 servings, at 110 calories each. Now, in the real world, who will drink just *one serving* of that bottle? Is it any surprise that many of us are super-sized ourselves?

5. **Check the calories per serving.**

All too many people think the "110 calories" posted on that 20-ounce bottle of cola means they are drinking 110 calories. Hardly. You have to multiply the 110 calories by the total number of servings, 2.5, to realize that you are actually downing a whopping 275 calories.

Don't get too comfortable with "0s" either. Because some manufacturers use ridiculously small serving sizes (remember that 120th of an ounce of cooking spray?) and because the FDA states that manufacturers can "round down" to zero, some products advertised as calorie-free or fat-free are not. If you eat multiple servings—if, for example, you coat an entire skillet with oil spray—you can be tallying up quite a few calories.

6. **Check the calories from fat.**

It's on the Nutrition Facts label. Unfortunately, it doesn't tell you "percent of calories from fat," which is how all health guidelines direct us to limit fat. You have to do a little math. Divide the number of calories from fat by the total calories. (If the serving's 150 calories, 50 of which are fat, your product has 33 percent of its calories from fat.).

If division trips you up, go by grams and use this easy rule. If a product has two grams of fat or less per 100 calories, its fat content is within Pritikin guidelines for processed foods: the fat, per serving, is 20 percent or less of total calories. You don't have to be a mathematician to realize that four grams of fat per 100 calories is double the fat recommended by the Pritikin Eating Plan.

Don't be fooled by claims, such as *99 percent fat-free* soup or *2 percent fat* milk. They are based on percent of weight, *not* percent of calories. So that can of 99 percent fat-free soup can actually have 77 percent of its calories from fat or more. And two percent fat milk actually has about 34 percent of total calories from fat; 1 percent milk has about 23 percent calories from fat.

7. **Check the sodium.**

Don't bother with the percentage of Daily Value (DV) of sodium. Don't bother with Daily Value percentages period. They are based on government standards, which are generally not as healthful as Pritikin Program guidelines.

Instead, look at the number of milligrams of sodium the serving contains. A great rule of thumb: Limit the sodium in milligrams to no more than the number of calories in each serving. Your daily goal: less than 1500mg of sodium.

8. **Check the types of fat.**

    Make sure there are no saturated fats, hydrogenated fats, or tropical oils in the ingredient list, including lard, butter, coconut, cocoa butter, palm oils, shortening, margarine, chocolate, and whole and part-skim dairy products.

    Polyunsaturated fats (such as safflower, soybean, corn, and sesame) and monounsaturated fats (such as olive and canola) are less harmful and would be acceptable, but make sure the percent calories from fat are still in line—20 percent or less of the calories from fat —or your waistline might start getting out of line. All oils, even "good" oils, are dense with calories.

9. **Check the sugar.**

    Limit caloric sweeteners. Watch out for sugars and other caloric sweeteners that don't say "sugar" but in fact are, such as corn syrup, rice and maple syrup, molasses, honey, malted barley, barley malt, or ingredients that end in "ol," such as sorbitol or maltitol, and ingredients that end in "ose," such as dextrose or fructose.

    Try to limit all these added, refined, concentrated sugars to no more than five percent of total calories (essentially, no more than two tablespoons daily for most folks). Don't be concerned about naturally occurring sugars in fruit and some nonfat dairy products. However, on the Nutrition Facts label, added sugars and naturally occurring sugars are all lumped together as "sugar."

    Your best bet: Look at the ingredient list. Try to avoid foods with added, refined caloric sweeteners in the first three to five ingredients. Because ingredients are listed in descending order of weight, the lower down the label you find added sugars, the better.

10. Make sure that any grain is *whole* grain, such as whole-wheat flour.

Many bread and pasta products claim to be whole wheat, but the first ingredient in the ingredient list is often wheat flour, which *sounds* healthy, but it's really *refined* flour. Further down the list will be whole-wheat flour or bran. Scout out products that contain only *whole* grains. And look for at least three grams of fiber per serving, which often ensures the product is mostly, if not all, whole grain.

If the product sounds too good to be true, it might be. Thousands of new products come out every year, many trying to cash in on the latest diet craze. As we've seen with the low-carb craze, many might not be carefully regulated (if at all). In 2001, the Florida FDA evaluated 67 diet products and found all 67 were inaccurately labeled; they contained more sugar and carbs than their labels stated. And recently, consumer laboratories evaluated 30 low-carb nutrition bars and found that 60 percent were inaccurately labeled. Most had more carbs, sugars, and salt than their labels claimed.

During your first few trips to the market, give yourself extra time to evaluate products. You'll soon speed up! After you find products that you enjoy and that meet these healthy guidelines, shopping becomes quick and easy. Your health is worth it!

▪▪ Dr. C. Everett Koop: The Nation's Top Doc

Many people remember Dr. C. Everett Koop as the U.S. Surgeon General with the funny bowties. However, he is also the man whom many say is largely responsible for reducing the number of smokers in the U.S. when he helped mandate the now ubiquitous Surgeon General's Warning on cigarette packs. Looking back, Dr. Koop rose to his most prominent role at a time when most people are ready to retire. After an illustrious career in academics as a pediatric surgeon, Dr. Koop was 66 by the time President Ronald Reagan appointed him the nation's top doc.

Now that Dr. Koop is 87, he's living proof that his views on aging well and staying healthy work. Like most doctors, he advises people to stay away from fad diets. He still exercises and has his entire life, even during those exhaustive resident years when doctors are on call every other day.

Knowing the risk of your mind turning to mush in retirement, Dr. Koop made sure to take up hobbies in his later years, one of which included the art of cutting semi-precious stones. He was so excited by this hobby that he stayed up for many nights until 1 a.m. cutting stones. The result was that years after he retired from pediatric surgery, Dr. Koop still had the eye-hand coordination many surgeons lose after they stop working. Dr. Koop continues to teach and conduct research as the senior scholar of the C. Everett Koop Institute at Dartmouth University. He relishes his mission to improve public health, writing numerous articles for academic journals and mass media. As we were researching exercising and eating right, we decided to catch up with Dr. Koop at his home in Hanover, New Hampshire to get his advice on aging well. As usual, he was colorful and direct. Here's what he had to say:

I was always active. When I was a medical resident, I used a pedometer. This showed I walked about 14 miles daily as I walked all over the hospital wings, and so on. When I was a surgeon even decades later, I still walked about half that.

One tip is to always walk down the stairs and walk up, too, except when there are too many flights. At the end of the day, I always walked up a few flights of stairs and then down to the street level. No matter what level you work on, build in a few trips up a few flights of stairs during the day. I can't prove it, but I truly feel that if I had not remained active, I would not be here to have a conversation with you.

But unlike the common advice, my answer is not just to keep active, for example, with hobbies or some light volunteer activities. My views go beyond this and are shaped by having observed colleagues who reached age 65 and were hurt at that time when the University just tells you there is no longer a role for you.

My key is that society has to have some expectation of you. I tell groups of seniors that I'm asked to lecture to make sure you give a full commitment. Don't say, "I'll help unless it's a good day for golf or unless I'm asked to babysit." Think about making a sincere time contribution to a community and stay active that way. The key is to be reliable—make a full commitment.

I've had typical exchanges with friends who retired at age 65 and my dialogue with them is roughly:

"Harry, what will you do after you retire?"

"Travel."

"Okay, you take three cruises and lose your bags four times, then what?"

"Grow roses in my garden."

"Okay, after you grow roses and give them to some ladies, then what?"

"Then I want to get a lathe and make pretty wood objects for the ladies."

"But, then what?"

I see as a truth, surgeons, sharp as tacks, hit age 65 in the spring, retire in June, and within two years they are just following their wives around the supermarket, arguing about which cereal to buy. By then, they are not even interesting to speak to—and they were brilliant surgeons.

Why does society tell us to retire at the same age as our ancestors when life expectancy has increased so much each successive generation? We now live so much longer that we can retire later and still be able to have long retirements.

Why believe you have to shuffle just because you reach a certain age? I always believed that on New York City sidewalks, I could go on year after year walking faster than most people and I did this until I just couldn't any more, but this was not until I was into my 80s.

I am convinced that a year exists for most people—for me it was age 85—when they really feel a bigger physical deterioration. When I was 84, I would see 64-year-old doctors go up to the podium to give a lecture and hang on to the banister to step up four stairs. I would think: "Is this guy really an expert on taking care of the body?"

However, it is true that with age goes balance. At some age— for me it was not until 85—it does pay to hold the banister as opposed to stumbling down the stairs.

But that one year came relatively late in a long and full life.

Keep away from fad diets. If I hear "What do you think of the grapefruit diet" or any diet X, I answer, "I don't know anything about it, but don't go on it!"

I get so mad seeing commercials that extol how low carb a beer is. Carbs alone are not the issue. A high-fat diet can be bad for the heart, kidneys, and so on. Dr. Atkins himself likely had terrible cardiac health and presumably ate his own Atkins Diet. Big deal if food has a red seal from the Atkins Commission. What objective scientific authority do they have?

Indeed, carbs are essential. They are the source of so many needed vitamins and nutrients. Low-carb diets that cut out or severely limit fruits and vegetables are unhealthy. The best advice is to follow the new work the Food and Drug Administration is doing on a balanced pyramid of food each day: carbs, protein, and the right fats in moderation. Gaining weight is a matter of more energy in than out, not what type of calories you take in. The best thing to do is to have a physician guide you—except medical schools need to do a better job teaching medical students more about nutrition. Many MDs find it a boring subject because it is not so glamorously high tech as some others, leading too many medical schools not to emphasize it enough. Nutrition is a personal thing, so you need a personal guide. That is, the guidance of a qualified nutritionist or a doctor who does take nutrition seriously.

I know I have been instrumental in postponing the deaths of many people by my early emphasis on reducing the nation's excessive smoking. To give a vivid and important example: getting all smoking off airplanes. When I fly now, flight attendants still lean over and thank me for that!

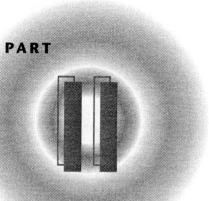

YOUR MIND

Taking Care of Your Brain

If you ask any aging person what one of the biggest things they worry about is, the person would probably say something along the lines of "losing my mind." To many of us, our mind represents the essence of our being. Dr. Johnnetta Cole, the energetic 69-year-old president of Bennett College told us candidly that her "biggest fear is that I will lose the capacity to be engaged mentally."

"Obviously, I don't look forward to physical infirmities, but the ability to read, to write, and to think are really very central to my sense of myself and to my happiness," she told us. To help cope with the ravages of mental stress, Dr. Cole told us she often flies to Paris to listen to her brother play jazz.

"He's a jazz drummer and one of the ways I relax and feel a great deal of enjoyment is by listening to black improvisational music, otherwise known as jazz. Going to a city that is totally intriguing and being there with my only brother who knows the world of jazz because it's his world—that's quite special."

You might say that people involved in academics are particularly sensitive to the thought of losing their minds as they age. They earn a living off of how primed they can keep this all-important organ. Doctors are quite aware of this as well. (See Dr. Koop's point about surgeons turning to intellectual mush after retirement.) You might occasionally encounter a doctor who smokes or is too fat, but you will rarely find one who isn't constantly reading up on the latest developments in his field or engaging in medical lectures and conferences. In addition, if you do encounter one who doesn't do these things, you better switch doctors.

It's fairly widely accepted that those who stay mentally challenged throughout their lives have a much better shot at *remaining* mentally sharp until the very end of their lives. Your brain is just like every other muscle in your body; if you don't use it, it'll get weak. It'll become more susceptible to wear and tear; the longer you stop exercising it, the harder it'll be to get it back into tip-top shape. If your brain is not kept running and stimulated, the dendrites—those tree-like extensions of a neuron that receive information from other neurons—actually atrophy. You literally lose mass.

Not many of us realize this, but our brains are malleable. Remember how you were told not to drink too much alcohol in college because you'd kill too many brain cells that don't grow back? Well, that's not entirely true. Neurologists are now finding that the brain actually can generate new cells even into older age, though not at such a great rate that you can maintain a constant number. Still, it means that our brains continue to grow. We can make it perform better. We can slow the decline.

That's good news for us as we age. It means we can have some control over whether we develop age-related dementia. When people say they don't want to lose their minds as they age, they mean they don't want to become the crazy old person who shouts at no one in particular in a nursing home. That's a fate worse than death for some people. After the mind stops functioning, the sense of self is gone. The whole reason why you are reading this book is because you not only want to be alive and kicking at 85, but also alive and kicking and fully functioning as *yourself*.

Now, remember that Alzheimer's, the severest form of age-related dementia, still affects only a small percentage of the older population—just 5 percent to 10 percent of American people over 65, depending on which study you quote.

But milder forms of dementia are more common and often a part of aging. Your brain, like everything else in your body, slows down over the years. No matter how much you exercise at age 55, you certainly don't expect to win any Hawaiian Tropic beauty pageants, right? The point is you're trying to do everything you can to stay fit as you age, but inevitably your triceps will jiggle like Jell-O no matter how many arm curls you do.

The same goes for your brain as you age. For some people, you may experience nothing more than a few episodes of "senior moments." Oops, you forgot where you put the car keys, or to unplug the iron, or to turn off the bathroom faucet. They're not real debilitating moments.

The important thing to know is if you're at this stage, or even if you're not, your job is to do everything possible to prevent it from reaching the *irreversible* stage: Alzheimer's. After you develop the disease, that's bad news for you. You can't do much about it. You need to right now put everything you can into making sure you never develop Alzheimer's by exercising your brain. You have to protect it as if it's the most valuable trophy in the world.

Are We Facing an Alzheimer's Epidemic?

As we, the authors, are an academic and a journalist, statistics provide the foundation of our work. However, we sometimes recognize that numbers can cloud the picture.

Take Alzheimer's, for example. There's no denying the incredibly urgent need to find a cure for Alzheimer's. According to the Alzheimer's Association, the number of people afflicted by the disease has doubled in the last 25 years to about 4.5 million people. In 45 years, that number could more than triple to nearly 16 million Americans (and a majority of Baby Boomers). Nearly half of people over 85 are affected by the disease, the association notes in its fact sheet.

Don't panic yet. The reason why we've seen such a huge surge in Alzheimer's is far more complicated than that we're suddenly experiencing a mysterious "epidemic." For one, we're living longer, which means many of us are approaching ages where the disease manifests, usually between ages 65 to 85. The more old people there are, the more likely you'll see people diagnosed with Alzheimer's.

We're also getting much better at diagnosing the disease. We understand better the way the disease works, how it affects us, when it begins cropping up. Forty years ago, the disease may have gone undetected until the last phase of development (which is what happened to Rita Hayworth). Now doctors are more frequently diagnosing Alzheimer's at far earlier stages.

Let's not forget the famous people we've seen affected by the disease, which enhances the public fear of Alzheimer's. Longtime sufferer Ronald Reagan passed away from the disease. Actor Charlton Heston, also known as Moses, revealed he was diagnosed with Alzheimer's in 2002. Sexy screen siren Rita Hayworth died in 1987 after living with the disease for more than 20 years (and which wasn't diagnosed until 1980). Seeing such larger-than-life figures debilitated by the disease, coupled with the frightening statistics, raises the fear that Alzheimer's is lurking around the corner for us.

This is not to say that you shouldn't be concerned with the disease. Its danger is very real and present, and you should do everything you can to make sure Alzheimer's does not find you. We give you ways to exercise your mind later in this section, which is one of the main ways to stall or prevent age-related dementia. But don't go into irrational fear mode and throw away your antiperspirants because you heard the aluminum in them is linked to Alzheimer's (the studies on this are highly inconclusive).

As important as staying mentally fit is keeping a good, healthy perspective.

The Alzheimer's Association has started a campaign to get everyone to build up "cognitive reserves," which is like backup ammo for your brain in case of attacks. If you do this, you might not even develop those mild senior moments. You might be the only 80-year-old on your block who knows exactly where you put the car keys.

There's a reason why more highly educated people have a lower rate of developing dementia or Alzheimer's. Or why it seems that many CEOs, scientists, and professors function at impressive mental speeds into their 70s and 80s. Barbara Walters, at 78, is still quick as a whip when it comes to the follow-up interview question. Federal Reserve chairman Alan Greenspan, at 78, held the world's most powerful position in the global economy. It's not luck. It's practice.

As mentioned, academics, researchers, executives—people who use their brains constantly to do their work—are always flexing their knowledge muscle. They keep the brain running in top form. You might hear these people talk about being "in the zone" when they're working, where they're so deeply involved in a complex mental task that they don't notice anything around them. Hours can fly by in minutes. It's like the runner's high— you exercise to the point that you reach a feeling of euphoria.

People engaged in this "zone" are experiencing a high-level form of "cognitive processing." It's when your brain is not just doing its automatic functions, but also analyzing, solving, multitasking, and so forth. The brain is being challenged. When you engage in cognitive processing, you improve your overall brain function. You make your brain healthier.

We'll get to the different ways you can keep your brain primed. You wouldn't think it would be this way, but it's just as much of a chore to exercise your brain as it is to exercise your body. How many of us would rather just plunk down in front of the television than learn a new skill? Researchers equate television watching with an *absence* of cognitive processing. When you watch television, you do nothing for the brain.

It's too simplistic to think that you can just do *The New York Times* crossword puzzles and you'll be okay. You also can't assume that if you're smart, you won't get Alzheimer's.

Like much of what we talk about in this book, keeping your brain in shape requires lifestyle changes. It requires the dreaded word *commitment*. More than that, it requires a different way of looking at life. It requires you to perhaps change some practices, even aspects of your personality that have been bad for you. The funny thing is you'll have to *think* about thinking.

What's the worse that can happen? You exercise the brain and stay sharp until you're 90 and make everyone else around you amazed?

On the other hand, you face the alternative possibility of years of forgetfulness and the constant worry you may develop Alzheimer's. Do something more for your brain than worry.

▄▄▄ Former President Jimmy Carter on Aging

Whenever President Jimmy Carter travels around America, inevitably a crowd of gentle, smiley-faced fans follow him. His fans are the kind of people who are now called "middle America," ordinary folks who admire President Carter's homespun persona.

Say what you will about his political beliefs or his presidency, Jimmy Carter is perhaps the only U.S. president who still stays so closely in touch with the American people. He works hard at it. On most weekends, you'll find him teaching Sunday school in his old stomping grounds of Plains, Georgia, that is, if he isn't out helping broker peace deals or monitoring democratic elections in rural China. He has written 20 books, and many of them have nothing to do with politics. One of his favorites is *Virtues of Aging*, a subject he knows much about now that he is well into his 80s.

His down-to-earth appeal rests against an incredibly accomplished background, culminating in his becoming the 39th president of the United States. However, it's the way President Carter lived his life after he failed to win a second term that endeared him to Americans. America loves a good comeback story, and Jimmy Carter's is one of the most well known—how the most powerful man in the world, battered and bruised from four turbulent years in the Oval office, reinvented himself as one of the world's most effective humanitarians, winning a Nobel Peace Prize and earning the respect of hundreds of millions of people around the globe.

In many ways, this book is about preparing for your own comeback. Later on, we discuss the virtue of embarking on several careers in your lifetime. Why? Because in this day and age, when corporations slash costs and cut jobs, trade young labor for old, eschew loyalty for budget cuts, it's a rarity to see workers employed with one company for 30 or 40 years. Some companies still value the long-tenured employee, and we applaud them for this (such as Hearst and Oreck), but chances are that at some point, you may find yourself at the cusp of every employees' nightmare: downsized, pushed out, "retired." Just like Jimmy Carter.

Even if you are one of the lucky ones to escape corporate restructuring, you will likely feel at some point in your life that your current position is not enough. Perhaps just as bad as being pushed out of a job is being *bored* with it. You risk becoming intellectually lazy. This is around the time people start fantasizing about opening that bed and breakfast in Martha's Vineyard.

Don't face this proposition with fear and trepidation. Even the most successful people go through this. Jimmy Carter very openly calls his failed re-election in 1980 a "firing." Your job is to prepare yourself, like him, for the comeback. How do you pick yourself up and move on?

We asked this of Jimmy Carter himself. Following is what he had to say:

Well, there are two ways to lose a job involuntarily. One is just to get fired or not re-elected as happened with us. That's one way, in an unplanned way, to have your job terminated.

The other way is just to reach mandatory retirement age, and that's a predictable event for which you have adequate time to prepare if you have the courage and ability and insight to do so. Foresight might be a better word.

As I licked my wounds and realized that I had maybe 25 years of life expectancy in front of me, I said to myself what in the world am I going to do with these enforced retirement years that will be, I'd say, interesting and gratifying and suited to my own priorities, but also would utilize to the utmost the talent or ability or background or experience that I have accumulated over the previous years of my life? And that's what we did—a very deep and penetrating and sometimes painful reassessment of what Rosalynn and I would do after the White House.

I think in general terms that's what everyone should do. I think that one of the most valuable books that I've ever written is Virtues of Aging. *Just showing that when you reach the age of retirement, either mandatory or involuntarily, it should be an opportunity to open your possibilities to things that, that perhaps in the past, you have really wanted to do and didn't have time.*

Retirement's a time for potential despair, and for some people who either reach mandatory retirement age or are fired, it is a time of actual despair, and sometimes people just fold their wings and say, "I have a hopeless and fruitless life ahead of me." All too frequently, that results in severe mental, clinical depression, or even suicide or even, you know, the initiation of physical illness that is brought about by not being willing to face the future with pleasure.

I think the main thing is to be innovative in assessing your talents, your abilities, your interests. Also, don't be too exclusive in giving credit to the opportunities that you already have. Some people are frustrated or close doors unnecessarily to their future exciting life just by not realizing what they have at home to do— what the opportunities are that they have at home. Almost anybody, for instance, can find a place to put up an easel or to have a small wood shop—in an attic or basement or in part of a garage. Obviously if you have a computer, you can write books or become a poet, or you can walk in nearby parks and look at birds and things of that kind. Or you can take on special studies, let's say, even studies of science or geology or things of that kind.

Even if you have a humdrum job, making hamburgers in a Burger King, or being a stenographer for a boss that's not inspiring and you consider it to be just a drudgery job, what you do outside working hours can be extraordinary. If you look at the time available in an average week—if you'll just mark off 40 hours for work—there are a lot of hours left over every week that can be used either for pure enjoyment or for challenging experiences or for productive contributions.

Except for entering and leaving the Navy, all my careers have overlapped, which is another point to be made. I'm still a farmer. I'm still something of a statesman. I'm still involved in writing books, and I'm still a professor. So, I think an important point to be made is that the [different careers] are not mutually exclusive. And sometimes, some of the most intriguing things that we do can be classified as hobbies.

For instance, if you live in a northern area, say on Fifth Avenue in New York or near Fifth Avenue, you can become a consummate bird watcher just by going to Central Park. If you live in an isolated place such as Plains, which has a total population of 635, there's nothing that will impede you in that narrowly confined environment from being a superb author or woodworker or painter or whatever you choose to do as an advanced hobby. You don't have to travel around to do it.

Constantly try to expand your heart and mind to encompass other people, other ideas, and other personal experiences. Those personal experiences—particularly just enjoying life—is an important part of anyone's career and they are enhanced by sharing those fun times with people that you care about, either close friends or your own family members.

I think that anyone—no matter what age they might be—should try to combine as much as possible their absolutely mandatory routine duties with as many ancillary interests, particularly enjoyable ones, as possible. Don't just be narrowly focused on one or two subjects—that might get very boring and frustrating as time goes on.

CHAPTER

Staying Curious

It's funny, but curiosity is a double-edged sword. On the one hand, it opens us up to amazing experiences. It's what makes us travel the world, take on new careers, or try some exotic food like snake soup. Some extremely curious people can't bear to go a day without learning something new. It's a part of their personal growth.

Then, curiosity can bite us in the rear. We try our hand at a new business and it fails. Or we start learning golf and realize we have the worst hand-eye coordination this side of the Mason-Dixon line. When examining happiness in people, psychologists have found curiosity as a positive and negative. It sometimes makes people happy and sometimes does not.

If you want to keep exercising your brain, curiosity is essential. It makes the wheels turn. Remember when you were a kid and the littlest things fascinated you? You would walk in the park and a strange-looking flower or bug might catch your eye, and before you knew it, you would sit there examining or playing with it for hours. Or you would ask your parents a thousand questions, all starting with the word "why." There's nothing like that internal *click* you get in your head when a mystery has been solved.

When you are a kid, curiosity comes easy. Your brain is developing rapidly; it's growing and getting bigger. Your appetite for new experiences flows naturally. The neurons in your brain fire left and right like the Fourth of July. You *want* to learn new sports. You *want* to know how things work. Babies are intensely curious creatures; they are driven to grow by their curiosity. Curiosity is the force behind our personal growth and development. When you are curious, your brain develops. Biologists sometimes point to curiosity as part of a survival mechanism. In primitive times, curiosity drove people to taste new plants or discover new territories, which was essential for survival. Imagine if our ancestors never had the curiosity to rub two twigs together.

A few people are lucky enough to retain this kid-like curiosity forever. However, most of us can get into a rut. As we age, this pure, natural curiosity becomes muddied. Other things occupy and clutter our minds. Stress puts a damper on curiosity—so do some bad experiences. Maybe you fail miserably at a business venture. The next time a similar opportunity comes around, you might think twice about it. You are afraid to go for it, and curiosity alone is not enough to get you over the hump.

If you are headed this way, be careful. You are in danger of heeding to that "voice." You know the one. The voice that tells you not to bother with starting new adventures because it would cause you too much trouble. The one that stops you from trying something new because you might fall flat on your face. It's the voice that talks you out of so many things that you eventually lose interest.

Did you ever notice that intensely curious people usually have an extra kick in their step? Curious people are not necessarily extroverts blazing through life at 110 mph. Often, they are quiet and introverted. They are humbled by their lack of knowledge and also driven by it. Curiosity exercises your brain, which in turn, makes you a healthier person.

So your job, as you age, is to put the shine back into your curiosity. Dust it off. Here's how.

▪▪▪ Learn New Skills

We won't get too psychoanalytical here, but we will say that curiosity is linked to a person's ability to be open to new experiences.

Although it's a toss-up as to whether it makes us happy, being open to new experiences is linked to people who seek intellectual or physical stimulation. They are the kinds of people who are always searching for something new. They want to expand their horizons, so to speak, even if it sometimes frustrates them. They are voracious readers. Or they travel incessantly. They are likely the ones to try out snowboarding at the age of 50.

We need to *flex* this personality trait. We all have it, but like anything else, it can get buried. You know the idiom "curiosity killed the cat." Sadly, some people live by this, afraid that trying something new will take them out of their comfort zone. We are not just talking about the physical stuff, such as suddenly delving into extreme sports in middle age. We are also talking about taking yourself out of your mental comfort zone.

To preserve your curiosity, you have to open yourself to new experiences. The best way to do this is to learn a new skill or a hobby. Start developing interests outside of work. Think back on the things, no matter how outrageous, you have always wanted to learn. Too often people look back and wished they had done this or that, traveled here or there, but didn't because they spent 60 hours a week at work. You know what that leads to? Burnout. And it's tough to be a curious person when you are burned out.

Earlier in this book, Dr. Koop explained that he picked up gem cutting after retiring as surgeon general. Several other people told us that they started a new hobby or skill just as they were retiring. Jimmy Carter began oil painting and now sells his paintings, along with his handcrafted wooden furniture, to benefit charitable programs to the tune of hundreds of thousands of dollars. Helen Gurley Brown, the legendary magazine editor, commissioned French lessons after she left her editorship of *Cosmopolitan* magazine. A friend of ours, a marketing executive at BellSouth, began learning the piano when she left her job.

These are people who intuitively know they need to tap into their curiosity to stay healthy. Something just doesn't sit right with them unless they learn new things and acquire new skills. They might not be so great at them, but that's not the point. They need to flex their knowledge muscle. We know what you might be thinking. You don't have time to start a new hobby right now. You have too many things to think about instead of learning gardening or horseback riding. Stop right there. That's the "voice" emerging. Tell it to take a hike.

Start small if you want. Curiosity doesn't come naturally for everyone. Start off by doing something easy, such as reading a new book. Think back on all those classics you did not finish in school. Pick one up again. Or join a nearby book club. You will get plenty of other benefits, such as socializing and friendships. The main thing is to do something you've never done before. Break the routine.

Wine for the Mind

You have probably heard how wine might be good for your health. Research points out how it might also be good for your brain.

Findings from the Rotterdam Study in the Netherlands, which has tracked men and women over age 55 living in Ommoord, a suburb of Rotterdam, since 1990, showed that moderate alcohol consumption lessened the risk of dementia, with the greatest benefit to those who possessed the Alzheimer's gene, APOE4.

Another study published in the *New England Journal of Medicine*, which followed women aged 70 to 81 years through 1995 to 2001, found that those who drank a 4-ounce glass of wine or a 12-ounce glass of beer a day showed better cognitive scores. The researchers noted red wine had the most protective effect against mental decline.

As living proof, we turned to Robert Mondavi, founder of the wildly successful Mondavi winery, who attributes his long, colorful life to the delectable grape.

"I feel wine has [helped me age well]," he told us. "And, I feel that drinking wine helps me live a balanced life. It makes me happier and gives me health benefits. I like all varietal wines, if they are made well."

The 92-year-old wine patriarch, who started from scratch forty years ago to build the winery that has now become legend in the Napa Valley, shared with us some other secrets to a long and successful life. Some of these you'll find in his own book, *Harvests of Joy*, which is a truly fascinating account of how he lost almost everything in his mid-50s, only to turn around years later to become an even bigger success by changing America's taste for wines. Talk about another comeback story. Enjoy it one evening with a nice glass of, what else, wine.

Mondavi's Secrets to Success:

- Have confidence and faith in yourself.
- Whatever you choose to do, make a commitment to excel and pour yourself into it with heart and soul.
- Interest is not enough—you must be passionate about what you do. I say, find a job you love, and you'll never have to work a day in your life.
- Establish a goal just beyond what you think you can do and learn to embrace risk.
- It is very important that we understand one another. Listen carefully and when you talk, be sure people understand you. On important issues, have people repeat back to you what you've said to make sure there are no areas of confusion or conflict.
- Always stay positive and remember this: America was built on the can-do spirit and will continue to thrive on the can-do spirit.
- The greatest leaders don't rule. They inspire.

We are not asking for any big-time commitments. We are asking you to change your old way of thinking. Break the habit. From this day on, start doing things that are different. Learn about subjects outside your realm. Take a night class on pottery. Go to a museum at least one weekend a month. Try cooking a new ethnic meal. Learn, learn, learn. Before you know it, you'll hear the *click, click, click* go off in your head like a shutterbug.

Here's the best part. You'll get even *greater* benefits if you learn something completely opposite of what you are used to doing. The point is to exercise different parts of your brain that lay nearly dormant. Researchers have found that when people use their brains in unusual ways, blood flows into different neural regions and creates new connections. You're flexing news parts, which creates a much healthier mind. If you're a real analytical person, say an accountant or financial planner, try learning how to paint. Exercise the right part of your brain. If you're a writer or artist, learn how to fix a car. It sounds odd, but you'll feel different. If you spend all day in front of a computer, learn how to ski. If you ski all day, learn how to write. You get the idea. The point is to stretch yourself to places you never imagined. Our tendencies are to do similar things over and over again because they are familiar to us. We pick the same types of people as our friends. We pick the same models of cars to drive. We wear the same hairstyle for years. Whenever you do the opposite, it makes a heck of a difference.

You'll start to see old things in new ways. That's the beauty of curiosity. It's literally like putting on those rose-colored glasses—everything around you will appear different.

■■■ Asking Why

Aubrey Garlington is the father of one of our dear friends. He's an accomplished academic musicologist who is 74 and still writing books and giving lectures. If you hear him speak, he doesn't sound like a guy in his 70s. He sounds young. There's a clearness in his throat. His voice doesn't "catch" on words.

When we asked Aubrey for one of his secrets to aging well, he immediately began talking about his innate curiosity.

I'm fortunate in one sense in that I was born with a natural curiosity. That curiosity can be obsessive at times. It drives my wife and children crazy, but I've always remained somewhat curious. I think it's a secret to keeping mentally alive. When I was teaching at my first teaching job—I got my doctorate and went to Syracuse University—I was always interested in music as a cultural phenomenon, and this was in an interdisciplinary humanities department. Syracuse had this foreign studies program. The first one they had was in Florence. So here I am; I was interested in 19th century history, more interested in French and German romanticism, when I had this idea. I could develop enough skills to teach art history and could go to Florence. That set me learning about the Southern renaissance. I went there in 1965–1966 and went back in 1972–1973. That experience set off interests in a whole series of new things that were very rewarding to me, aesthetically and historically. That's the kind of thing where curiosity rewards you. I've always looked for new things. I think that has to do a great deal with aging well, but I haven't seen too many studies on this. I have curiosity naturally, but I think you can develop a sense of interest in the other [things outside your "self"].

I have so much curiosity that, in my own case, I sometimes think I could have probably done well with less. I'm in a very specialized field, and I've gone through to the end of it, but sometimes, I found myself getting sidetracked because I discovered some new thing that's so fascinating, I can't get back to my main project. But curiosity is very rewarding at this life stage that I'm in. I'm always thinking why is this? What is this? In terms of traveling with my wife, which I love to do, I'm constantly noticing new things and people doing things that I don't know a great deal about. What is that? Why is that there? Who is that? Even small things like flower arrangements. Why does that have to be arranged this way?

One of the most interesting books I've read, it's not a guide to life, but it's a very famous book, The Education of Henry Adams. It's an autobiography, a memoir, and it's a fascinating book. At one point, Adams makes a comment, after various things have happened to him, where he described himself as "knowing enough to be ignorant." He was always well aware there was something he didn't know and knowing that he was ignorant kept his mind open. I read this when I was in my 30s, and it struck me as a remarkably wise kind of thing. Knowing enough to be ignorant consciously helps keep the mind open. I used his quote in my lectures.

As we age, we lose the tendency to ask why. Toddlers can drive us nuts sometimes with their incessant "Why is the sky blue?" questions. But they're an important part of learning. We shouldn't suppress the urge to ask why. Asking why is an important part of opening ourselves to new experiences.

Aubrey has this gift of asking questions naturally. Our job is to ignite this "cognitive process" again. It sounds simple, maybe too easy, but it takes some effort. Ever been to a meeting and when the boss asks, "Any questions?" nobody raises a hand? For many people, asking why is like admitting you don't know anything.

> "I have no special talents. I am only passionately curious."
>
> —Albert Einstein

One thing you learn in journalism is there's no such thing as a stupid question. If reporters went around hesitating about what question to ask, you'd never get any news. Unfortunately, there are people in this world who think there is such a thing as a stupid question. These people suppress the urge to be curious.

You have to persist in asking questions about the things around you. You need to maintain that kid-like curiosity to keep stimulating your brain. There's a good reason why a disproportionate amount of medical researchers and scientists work into their very old ages. Science is a product of human curiosity. Curious people enter the field because they are always asking why. They have burning questions and they want answers. The questions don't stop when they hit retirement age; they continue because it's part of who they are.

You will do yourself—and your brain—a favor by remembering to ask why. Don't get obsessive about it. Just make it a point to tell yourself to ask questions. You might end up learning a few things.

▨ ▪ Helen Gurley Brown: Legendary Editrix and the Original Sex and the Single Girl

Quite simply, Helen Gurley Brown is proof that women get better with age. She's an inspiration to millions of women who incessantly fret that life heads downhill after 30. For years, in the pages of her magazine, *Cosmopolitan*, and through her wildly successful books, including the classic *Sex and the Single Girl*, Helen Gurley Brown has taught women how to be smart, successful, and sexy all at the same time.

She's also a role model to millions of Americans who find their true passion late in life. Ms. Brown didn't even begin the job and career she's best known for—editor-in-chief of *Cosmopolitan*—until she was well into her 40s!

Despite her lifelong message for women to live wild and independent lives, Helen Gurley Brown herself has been married to the same man, Hollywood movie producer David Brown, for more than 40 years. That marriage, however, came at the end of a string of failed relationships with several "Don Juans," which Helen Gurley Brown describes in vivid detail in her memoirs. Nobody would say Ms. Brown hasn't, at the age of 83, had her share of life experiences, both exhilarating and excruciating.

There's little doubt women and men view aging differently, though it's not as if one sex or the other deals with it better. If there's one universal truth, it's that nobody likes to age. As Helen Gurley Brown told us, the factors that have helped her age well work for anyone—man or woman. A strong marriage. Intellectual stimulation. Regular exercise. That and some expensive signature fishnet stockings can't hurt!

I guess in my whole life, I never thought about being older, just doing the best I could with what I had. Now that I am older, I'm trying to do the best I can. I cope and I'm not thinking about 104 or 109 or 99. I'm just thinking, "How can I be the best 83-year-old person I can be? How can I hang on?" I've got a big splash of nail polish on my wrists to remind me to stand up and sit up straight.

I'm not athletic. I'm not real strong. If I can exercise, then goodness knows anybody else can. It's such a necessity the older you get. Exercise is one of the things you know you can do to continue to feel okay. It means you can eat a little more and not be quite so scrupulous about calories. Every morning I hit the floor. I do half an hour of exercise and watch Good Morning America. *I'm not any good at it. I have these 7-pound weights—I've gone down from 10—that I can barely lift, but I do. I do push ups and sit-ups. My push ups—they're kind of fake. I do them on my knees and sometimes, I do get the knees off the floor. The sit-ups, I can do those with the hands behind the head. I didn't do all this when I was young. I wasn't a good athlete, nobody wanted me on their basketball or dodge ball team, but somehow, in my 40s, I had a girlfriend who had an exercise regimen she got in the mail. You paid $25 to get it, and I studied that. In my 40s, I began to exercise and now at 83, I must say, I don't miss a day.*

You have to live a reasonably healthy life and that means having to go to sleep every night. I sleep eight hours. I exercise. And you can't be an alcoholic. In terms of nutrition, I don't have a lot to learn because I know it all in my head. I've known for many years you need seven grams of protein, and you also need your fruits and veggies, and I don't always do it. Carbohydrates are bad, and you need to keep those at an absolute minimum.

If there's anything in the world I love it is cookies. I know about healthy eating and I don't always follow it, as I should, because I'm a cookie-holic. I pick up cookies left on a plate at the Four Seasons. I dump them in my purse. I enjoy French brownies enormously—how can I deny myself this great pleasure?

People often ask me about my long marriage. David [Brown] was married twice before. I didn't marry him until I was 37. I married a good person, a nice, decent, wonderful person. He's good to other people. He's got good character and he's a fine human being. When you go home at night, that's good for whatever is bothering you. You tell him about it. If somebody in your life loves you and believes in you and is supportive, how could you not be happier and more comfortable? I have had love affairs with some men that if I married, I would be dead by now. I was nuts about this Don Juan and I got lucky that he didn't marry me. Thank goodness! Some of those men I would have married would have made me miserable. I'm glad I met the right one. David is responsible for my jobs, my books, and my magazine. There's no question that having a good loved one in your life makes you happier and helps you live longer.

He wrote me a valentine last night. He can't rhyme, but it said, "From the time you were in the nursery/I knew you'd be mine/for better or worsery." He always writes me valentines and birthday poems and makes me read them out loud.

He didn't have a penny when I married him, and I had $8,000 in my savings account. He had no money whatsoever. He worked hard and made money each year, and now we're comfortable financially. We don't have a country house. We don't own an airplane. We don't have a boat. We don't want those things. We live comfortably. I took David with me to a Hearst conference, and he waited for me at the Claridges [hotel]. We got on a train and went through the Chunnel and went to Paris. He loves Paris. I went with him to be a good wife. They have incredible restaurants. I did that to humor David. It was sexy and romantic, and we drank champagne every night. I guess we deserve it. David is 88 and I'm 83. We've both worked hard, both helped other people. I took care of my mother and sister all the years of their lives. My husband has always taken care of other people.

David and I both think work is rewarding. There's a lot of good stuff that comes from working—it brings you recognition, respect from friends, self-esteem, and money, so those rewards are not thrown away. David has a wonderful play opening up on Broadway. People who've seen it in previews just rave about it. It looks like it might work. MGM asked him to look over a list of *movies to find anything that might be turned into a play, and he liked this particular movie* Dirty Rotten Scoundrels. *He's almost 89 years old. Most men don't have the courage to do that, to raise money. He had to raise millions and that's not easy.*

I'm a good example of what can happen without any college education. I succeeded just from doing what I could. There's always something you can do better than other people. If you arrange flowers, you can work for a florist and one day get your own flower shop. If you cook, you can work for a restaurant and become a manager and then maybe start your own restaurant. It doesn't matter what your specialty is, maybe it's children. You can start a preschool group; something out there can always be developed. I didn't feel I had to know when I was 17 what I was good at for the rest of my life. Get in to college if you can but just keep exploring. Keep talking to people.

Everything good that has happened to me is because I just got up in the morning and did it. Whatever I was supposed to, I did it because I had to. I didn't have any options. When I was 15, my sister got polio, and she was plopped into a wheel chair. I had no options except to support the family. They couldn't send me to college. I quickly had to learn shorthand and to type, and as soon as I learned those skills, I got a secretary job. I had 17 secretary jobs, one after the other, and I usually got fired. But I moved on a little bit to make more money, and my point is that I guess I feel devoutly that you should just get up and do it, do what you have to do, do the best things you can, do the tough stuff first.

A few years ago, when I came back from vacation, the CEO of Hearst was sitting in my office. I thought, "What is he doing here? He doesn't have an appointment." He said to me, "Maybe it's time to think about a younger editor for Cosmo." I said, "What's wrong? I'm only 76 years old!" He said they would give me two years to work with her. If I thought she was the one, maybe she could take charge. It was very generous. We started the two-year run, and I knew in the first two weeks she'd be terrific. At the same time, I knew I would go out the window if I didn't have a job of some kind.

They were very gracious. They said I could be in charge of the international editions. At the time, there were about 19 or 20 editions. Next week, I'm going to Oslo to open up the 56th. But you see, this is a private company. In most companies, if you're 65, you're out the door. They don't want you anymore. Because Cosmo did so well for the company, it was the biggest money-maker, bigger than the TV stations, newspapers, and other magazines, they said let's keep her happy. But this international division, it does make money. It isn't just charity or philanthropy.

I'm lucky because I feel that I've paid my dues. I took care of my invalid sister and mother. I paid my dues in some tough jobs—some of the secretarial jobs were scruffy but I did what I needed to do. By the time I got to be 80, I'd done everything. I'd been around the world several times. I had written five, six books. I didn't have anything that needed to be done, didn't need any weekends to go visit the Met or the Museum of Natural History. The one thing I wanted to do was to learn French, so I started taking lessons when I stopped being the U.S. editor of Cosmo.

I've always adored clothing. My mother was a seamstress and always made wonderful clothes for me. I had beautiful clothes. She could afford a yard or two of fabric, and she could make me a dress. I've always loved fashion. Now I can afford to look pretty good, but I tend to be thrifty. It's hard to spend $3,500 on a Chanel suit. I do that once in a while. I try to look nice. Today, I wore a handknit red dress for Valentine's Day. I have good legs, so I can wear short dresses.

David Brown on Helen:

A great marriage has kept me alive. Helen gives me a reason to live, a wife who would not tolerate me retiring. I gain from my wife's concern for what I eat, what I drink, and that I exercise. We love each other, and that's that. It's a heck of a reason.

Sure I'm 89, but I come into the office every day, same as when I was 40, no difference. Age 65 for me was the beginning of adolescence. My wife and I each work at least eight hours every weekday and often into the weekend. We have been fortunate financially for a long while, but we don't have things such as a country house. We work in Manhattan and live here.

It is important to use your brain in many ways. I write articles for publications, such as Town & Country. *We both teach at Stanford every summer. I have always been interested in live theater.*

I exercise every day, and because I fractured a hip, I do Tai Chi to improve my balance. I watch my diet. The key is not eating a lot. We eat everything, but moderately.

Why do we keep working hard? Because we enjoy it more than we would enjoy hobbies. After guiding Cosmopolitan *for more than 30 years, they asked Helen to ease back and look into international editions. She started growing these editions and now there are 56! Helen always says, "I'd jump out the window if I didn't have a job." She is still working seven days a week as if our rent depended on it!*

When you ask about a favorite among the films I have produced, they are all my children. I am most proud of The Verdict. Jaws, *of course, set us financially.*

You ask my advice for those who would like to be doing well at nearly 90. Save your money. Watch your diet. That is, watch your wallet as well as your waistline. Study your craft, learn, and improve continuously. You have to keep moving. As the great pitcher Satchel Paige said, "Don't look back. Something might be gaining on you."

Marry well, not in terms of riches, but friendship as well as love and passion.

Practice Optimism

There's a man in Bologna, Italy named Giovanni Fava. He's a psychiatrist who runs a mental health clinic at the University of Bologna. Dr. Fava's a great guy, and he's done something you might like to know about. He's found a way to make people happier.

He calls it "well-being therapy." Basically, Dr. Fava takes patients recovering from depression and applies this therapy over the course of eight weeks. His objective is to make sure the patients don't go back into depression again—a relapse. The therapy mainly consists of patients writing down "well-being" events in a diary; for example, if they went to see their uncle the other day and received some gifts. That's a well-being event. Dr. Fava told us that it's odd at first; most patients, because they have been in the depths of depression for so long, look horrified when he gives them this task because they can't recognize when well-being events happen.

Over the two months, Dr. Fava and his team of therapists examine the diaries and invite the patients to focus on what the well-being events mean. He forces them to think about the event, which is cognitive processing. For example, they reflect on what it means when they receive the gifts or why they feel it's just luck that they had a good day at work. You get the picture.

Traditional therapy—think Tony Soprano on the couch—focuses on the patients' problems. Dr. Fava focuses on the patients' successes. The common strategy in traditional therapy asks "the patients to monitor episodes of distress and work on those. Here, you ask patients to monitor episodes of well-being and you work on those moments," he explained.

What happens then? The attitude of the person changes. It's not so much the problems go away, but that the person's ability to deal with the problems changes. "It's the attitude toward things in life, toward stresses, both good and bad," Dr. Fava says. His patients are learning the value of optimism. Six years after well-being therapy, Dr. Fava proudly notes most of his patients are still free from depression.

In this book, we talk about how curiosity fuels cognitive processing. It's like the gas in a car. It makes your brain run. Optimism works differently, but its function is the same. Think of optimism as the other fluids in your car that keep the machine performing at the highest level. Curiosity fuels the brain; optimism is the condition that makes your brain run the best.

Makes sense, right? When you're depressed, anxious, or stressed out, it's hard to focus on tasks. You might indulge in bad behaviors, such as drinking too much or procrastinating. Optimistic people can take on undesirable challenges because they see the light at the end of the proverbial tunnel. They have better coping skills. They often perform at top speeds because they have confidence in their abilities.

Your task, as you age, is to practice optimism to keep your brain functioning at its best. No matter how smart you are, if you are depressed, anxious, or unhappy, your mind will perform subpar.

Optimism has other benefits. It will help you keep stress at bay and cope with challenges. Optimism is essential to aging well.

Age Smart Tip: Write It Down

At first, writing in a diary sounds like something a teenage girl does in her bedroom, scribbling eager thoughts about her crushes. Then, we started to read some research, and go figure. Far from embarrassing, "journaling" is very much a useful and respected form of cognitive processing.

Scientists have discovered that journaling, or "written disclosure," can be as helpful for the mind as meditation. It can also improve our health. In one study, college students writing down their thoughts and feelings about traumatic events visited campus health clinics less often than their nonwriting classmates.

Other studies have found that patients afflicted with an immune-related disease who kept their thoughts in a journal saw an improvement in their condition.

Start keeping a journal. Start writing down your thoughts, your feelings, your dreams, and your observations in your journal. Try to write in it every day, if not every week. Or even try for once a month. The important thing is that you write things down. Make sure no one can read it. You will be more uninhibited that way. This is not a memoir. You don't need to write as if it will be published one day.

Writing is therapeutic, there's no question about that. It also forces us to take stock of the events in our lives, to think about the way we feel and the opinions we have. It's a form of self-analysis that eventually triggers questions and thoughts about the purpose of our lives. Don't just write about emotions, especially negative ones. Writing down your thoughts is healthy, unless you only dwell on negative feelings without analyzing them through cognitive processing. One study at the University of Iowa found that psychology students who wrote only about feelings concerning a tragic event fell ill more often than those who wrote about their feelings and what they learned from the event. So dig deeper than "I feel bad."

Go out and buy yourself a nice, bound notebook. Or, if you prefer, start posting on your own blog, those online web journals that are all the rage (but that, of course, takes away from your privacy). Whatever the form, the important thing is that you write. The bonus is at the end of it all, you will have a nice library of your thoughts, your memories, and your feelings. It might even save you a few bucks on the therapy couch.

It doesn't come easy—none of the suggestions we describe can happen at the snap of your fingers. Psychologists observe that many people have a natural tendency to dwell on negative events and emotions. Psychologists have even come up with a ratio—2.9 positive events have to happen to balance out every one negative event for us to be well. You have to work against natural habits. The following sections describe some ways to help you.

▪▪▪ Get Eight Hours of Sleep

This first suggestion is one of the easier ones, but it's one of the most important. Did you know that many adults get less than six hours of sleep a night when they should really get eight hours? Sleep is the one thing we sacrifice too easily in our adult years. There are all sorts of terrible things that happen to your body when you don't get enough sleep, but for this chapter, we focus on just one: your state of mind.

You have probably noticed that babies tend to get cranky if they don't get enough sleep. Ask any new mother and she will tell you how important naps and nighttime sleep are for her baby. That's the time when the little ones are growing. We experience the same benefits, though, of course, to a different degree.

We sleep in two parts. The first part is actually made up of four stages, but for simplicity's sake, just know that in the first hour or so of rest, you're going from a dozing-off stage to a deeper relaxed state where your breathing slows down. Doctors call this last stage "delta," or slow wave, sleep.

Once you're deep in sleep, you enter the Rapid Eye Movement (REM) part where it appears as though you are watching a NASCAR race with your lids closed. This stage helps preserve cognitive function, making sure you don't lose any benefits of all that brain-flexing you experienced during the day.

We cycle through these two stages over the course of a night. Delta, REM, delta, REM, delta, REM, delta. The longer you sleep, the more time you spend in the REM stage, which is crucial in helping your brain recuperate from the stresses of the day. If you don't get enough of this cycling, your brain gets off course. It gets stressed. Invariably, we become stressed. We get moodier. Studies show people who don't get enough sleep become depressed more easily. Even one night of sleep loss raises our stress hormone (cortisol) level until the next night.

If we could, we would make you take an afternoon siesta, too, because that also helps your brain grow. Our culture tends to pride itself on being wide awake, 24 hours a day. There's a bravado attached to all-nighters. Doctors take calls for 48 hours straight, no sleep. Can't handle it? Get out of the profession. The same goes in business. Any executive doing international trade will take calls at one o'clock in the morning. It's insane! We can't change those patterns right away—our work ethos is what makes this country so productive and efficient; however, we can tell you to get at least the minimum you need to remain healthy, vibrant, and happy. Remember, the older you get, the more you need the sleep.

By the way, if you are plopping down on your pillow and conking out in 30 seconds, you are not getting enough sleep. This means you are exhausted.

▪▪▪ Turn it On and Off

A friend, Josie, who is a software developer in Pasadena, California, described what happened one recent evening. She came home to find her husband irate about a little scheduling mix-up at work. For 45 minutes (and she kept track), her husband Dan stewed about the problem. Josie could almost see the steam whistling out his ears. Finally, she told him to think about the problem for 30 seconds more and then stop. No more. Shut it off. It worked, and Dan finally refocused on helping with dinner.

Of course, his problem didn't go away in 30 seconds, but his ability to cope with it improved. Rather than replaying the issue a hundred times in his head, Dan swept it away using a technique Josie thought of because she needed him to wash the lettuce.

Your coping techniques might vary from Josie's, but the concept is the same; you need to know how to turn off those negative thoughts. Remember optimism is not about being happy.

It's an attitude. It's a coping mechanism. It's a view of life. It's not that optimists are always happy, extroverted people. It's that they can deal with life's challenges in a positive, confident way.

Jan Leschly is a perfect example of someone who has this on-off ability mastered. He's the former CEO of SmithKline Beecham and was, in his 20s, one of the world's top-ranked tennis players. Jan is a total optimist. He talks a little like Wolfgang Puck, the celebrity chef, except Jan's accent is Danish. He has the same appealing, friendly personality and loud, inflected voice. Because of his tremendous success in both tennis and business, Jan is often asked to talk to other professional tennis players. He assures them that there's life after the sport. Often, he talks about two things he learned from playing tennis.

One is the importance of keeping score—that is, staying competitive. That's one secret to success.

The other key is to possess an expert ability to turn on and off. "Tennis puts you in a situation where you have to be totally focused and concentrate for five, ten seconds," Jan explained. "Then you have to be totally relaxed for 20 seconds. Then on for five, ten seconds, then relaxed. It goes on for four hours like that, on-off, on-off. When I'm at a meeting and I'm sitting there, I'm totally focused, totally concentrating. I never miss a beat. I never close my eyes at a meeting. After I get out of the meeting, I'm totally relaxed. I'm a totally different person. This on-off ability means I've never had a sleepless night. I can sleep anywhere. I can sleep in a car. I can sleep in a plane. I never wake up at 3 o'clock in the morning. I've never had a sleepless night. I think if you checked around and asked what other people had to say about me, the one thing they would say is Jan has never been stressed. My mood never changes. Nobody's ever seen me depressed because I'm very level. I never raise my voice; I never yell or get steamed. On the court, it's all about killing the guy. Off the court, I'm totally relaxed. Completely." Jan told us more about how to maintain a vibrant, active lifestyle after retirement, which you can read in the following sidebar.

Jan Leschly: Former CEO of SmithKline Beecham and World-Ranked Tennis Player

I think it's unhealthy not to be active. The fundamental issue you're raising, I totally support. People should go on, they should work. When trying to avoid Alzheimer's, people should do all sorts of exercises with the brain, keep working, keep getting excited. I find that absolutely necessary. I see that in my own life. When I was supposed to be retired at 60 from SmithKline, I found it ridiculous. I found I was not ready to retire at all. I was forced to do it. I said, "Jan, you're never going to retire. I have to do something different."

I was worried. When you've done a job that I've done, that I have had for 30 years, working for a major corporation, the person who people see has a lot of influence, a lot of resources, and a lot of perks. You have your own airplane, your own this and that, and then from one day to another, you're not in that office. You're not having the perks. You're not having the power, which is obviously addicting to some people. On that basis, what are you going to do?

I fortunately planned for it. How can I in any way utilize my expertise from the last 30 years? My son Mark, who at the time—this is now three and a half years ago—had experience in the venture capital industry. He was a partner in a venture capital fund at the age of 28 and now he's 37. He has enormous experience and he said, "Why don't you do [venture capitalism]? They could use your expertise. Use your network to build the team. You can have a lot of fun that way."

It's not been easy for me. There's been a learning curve. Look at how many CEOs start off saying, "I'm going to go on vacation, have a nice time and travel," and after a short period of time, end up being not nearly as energetic and active. It's a problem. In my case, yes, you're right, I'm totally privileged. But let me enjoy my summer house in Nantucket? That's not me.

I used to be the one who looked at presentations, said yes and no, signed off. In this case, as a VC, I have to go out and raise money, being on your knees, going where the money is, meeting after meeting after meeting. It's a humbling experience because you're not a CEO there. You're not a big shot. You're not the CEO of a major corporation. You're a partner in a capital venture fund and now you have to perform.

People ask me, "What are you doing?" They say, "Jan, you obviously don't have to do this." I tell them that it's not a matter of money; it's a matter of getting excited, using your intellectual power. Money does not drive me, but I've always felt money is a measure of success.

In life, you have inflection points. The you-have-to-make-a-decision points. I was a tennis player, made a lot of money. I realized if I didn't make a change in job or career, I would be stuck as a tennis player. The life cycle of a tennis player is very short. I realized if I didn't use the education I had and go into the business, I would be stuck as a tennis player into my mid-30s. At the age of 31, I made a major step. The last two tournaments I played back in 1971, I won the South African championship, I won $10,000, and then I won doubles for $3,000. That was $13,000 in a week. Then I went to Buenos Aires and played the finals in the South American championship. I made $5,000. Now I had $18,000. That was in 1971, so it was probably worth $100,000 in today's dollars. I went back to Denmark and never played a professional tournament since. Instead, I got a job in the pharmaceutical industry as assistant to the vice president of marketing. I found out you work from 8:00 a.m. to 4:30 p.m., take a half an hour lunch, and get $15,000 a year. That hurt. I was looking out the window, thinking, "Jan, what are you doing here? You were making all that money." But at the same time, something said to me, "Your wife and family will be ruined if you continue." You have to have rhythm in your life, you have to have consistency, you have to accept it. That's what I call an inflection point, you make an important decision.

I don't believe in miracle pills, but we'll make continuous progress in drugs. People say, "When are you going to find a cure for cancer?" There are 15, 20, 30 different types of cancer with different types of medications to treat each one. We'll start to move forward with genomics, stem cell therapy, but it'll be the next 10 to 20 years, not tomorrow.

In 1993, there was a grant from the NIH to develop [a map of the] genes and their impact on diseases. It was the human genome project. The guy who was an investor in all this, Wally Steinberg, had invested $70 million to buy the rights from the NIH to sequence all these different genes. I remember sitting at SmithKline Beecham, I said to myself, "This is going to change the world." The person in R and D [research and development] said to me that the only way to make a deal is if you go out and play tennis with Wally Steinberg. He was a complete tennis buff. He had his own coach, so I go out and play tennis and we make a deal. I acquired all of this.

During this conversation, I said, "Wally, what do you think really will be the huge impact of this?" He said, "Jan, this is what I expect. When I'm 186 years old, I'll play singles at Wimbledon center court." He died at 61, so he never saw the whole thing, but I'm just telling you, this guy had a vision.

How old do I feel? I have no idea. I feel good. I don't really care about it. I'm still going out for another fund, investing in it over the next 10 years, and I never think about the fact that I will be 74 by then. I enjoy every day now. The reason why I enjoy life is I have something to do that excites me.

As you age, your goal is to work on this on-off ability with your emotions. You can do it in a variety of ways. Some people count to 10 and let the anger or frustration subside. Other people go for a walk or think about something positive that happened recently. Some people picture a pleasant scene—maybe the beach. Do whatever works for you.

Try meditation. People who have practiced meditation all their lives, such as Tibetan Buddhist monks, have an uncanny ability to switch emotions as if they were changing television channels. One minute they can be serious, the next roaring with laughter. Infants are the same way. One minute they could be wailing and if you tickle them, they giggle. On-off. On-off. It seems strange to us, but this ability to change emotions quickly is a sign of a stress-free mind.

You have heard the refrain before. Don't let your emotions get the best of you. Now practice it.

■■■ Exercise, Exercise, Exercise!

Okay, so we circle back to our previous suggestion to get up off that couch and exercise! This, however, just drives home the thesis of this book—everything is interrelated. You can't look at all the different areas of your life as stand-alone compartments. Your finances affect your health. Your health affects your soul. Your body affects your mind. It goes on and on. Exercise is not just about tuning up your body. It's to help your brain, your attitude, and your entire being.

There's medical proof that exercising your body does wonders for your brain. Just as exercising preserves muscle mass, it also slows the loss of brain tissue common in aging. Exercise pumps up blood to your brain. Ever notice how alert and alive you feel after exercising? All that aerobic activity is getting the blood flowing through your veins and into your brain at a greater rate and volume.

One study showed that older adults who did moderate aerobic exercise, such as walking, performed better at executive tasks, such as problem solving, than those who didn't exercise at all. In research on rats and primates, scientists have found that exercise helps increase a substance in the brain called GDNF (short for "glial cell line-derived neurotrophic factor"). Doctors have explored infusing GDNF into the brains of patients with Parkinson's disease in order to keep them from losing brain function. In animal studies, scientists have found that by just exercising alone, GDNF increased four-fold! Yet another compelling reason to get moving.

Exercise does so many good things for your brain, and we are only now making the connections. For years, doctors have urged their older patients to start or increase their weight training because one of the leading causes of sickness and death in the elderly is falling. Doctors want us to strengthen our bones and muscles so we can walk down a flight of stairs without acting as though we are balancing on a tight rope. Medical research is beginning to delve into how exercise is linked to dementia.

First, a little background. Recent research has shown a link between diabetes and Alzheimer's. Diabetes, as you might know, is a disease that affects millions of Americans and is characterized by a resistance to insulin, which is essentially the hormone that helps your body process glucose—an essential source of energy.

Doctors began to see that many of their patients who had type 2 diabetes—the more common type in adults—were developing Alzheimer's. Studies were done and showed that when a patient has too much insulin coursing through the body, the enzyme that normally helps rid the body of this extra insulin becomes overloaded. The enzyme is so occupied with flushing out the insulin, it forgets to do its other job, which is to get rid of beta amyloid plaques that build up in the brain that lead to dementia and Alzheimer's.

This research is still in the preliminary stage, but the argument for exercise is compelling. What is one of the best ways to lower insulin resistance to help your body absorb insulin better? Exercise. All diabetics, if they want to control their disease, must exercise.

This is a perfect example of how exercise can benefit your brain in different ways with the same ultimate goal: preserving your mind. Exercising helps directly stimulate the brain, but it also keeps your physical health in shape so that you don't develop conditions, such as diabetes, that lead to dementia.

What's all this got to do with being optimistic? Well, other than the great things it does for your body, study after study has shown that exercising improves our psychological outlook. When you feel better about yourself physically, your emotions follow suit. You know the spring in your step after an hour of yoga or weight-lifting, right? Exercise relieves stress. It takes your mind off problems. As we discussed in this chapter, it makes your brain work better. There are many compelling reasons to stay physically active, and it's a shame we don't do it more often.

Don't limit yourself to just the gym. Walking is good exercise. So is housework. Or babysitting your grandchildren. Whatever makes you break a sweat gets your body pumping. Your body can't tell if you are lifting a barbell or your 20-pound grandson. The point is, and this goes for the rest of the advice we've given, to just do it!

■■ Zig Ziglar: One of the Country's Best Motivators

Though Zig Ziglar is fast approaching 80, he still travels all over the country, motivating millions of people to be the best at what they do. He holds court in football stadiums and concert arenas, talking for hours on end with the kind of energy that makes you tired just watching him. This same energy and drive has made his books, such as *See You at the Top* and *Over the Top,* bestsellers. (Go to www.zigziglar.com for a complete listing of Zig's books.)

Many people scoff at so called self-help gurus primarily because quite a few have been revealed as frauds. They often fail to "walk the talk." The secret to Zig's success is that he genuinely represents what he teaches. He is, as the saying goes, the "real deal." People sense this, which is why tens of thousands pack into stadiums to hear him speak.

The fact that he is 79, in wonderful health, bouncing from airport to airport making 50 speeches a year while still keeping close to his family shows that Zig is living life right. He's living his own secrets to success. If anyone can tell us how he's managed to age so well, it's Zig. Read on and see what he had to say.

Many people are amazed at the amount of energy I have, and, yes, I really do have a great deal of energy. Some ask how I can maintain that energy since I travel a lot, but I travel quite easily and I never just "sit there to get there." On my way to engagements, I am always either reading something I need to know, preparing my next presentation, or taking a nap or having a meal. I get there, unless it's an unusually long flight, in about the same condition I was in when I left.

I recognize that much of my energy is a gift. When I was 25 years old, I weighed 225 pounds, and when I got serious about life, after my encounter with Christ, I realized fully that my body was the temple of my soul, and that's when I got on a serious exercise and eating program. Interestingly enough, at age 45 in 1972, I weighed well over 200 pounds, and when I went to the Cooper Clinic [see the interview with Dr. Kenneth Cooper] for my treadmill test, my results were not spectacular, to say the least. At age 74, after these years of exercise and sensible eating, I actually stayed on the treadmill longer than I could when I was 45, overweight, and out of shape.

One thing that enables me to have a great deal of energy is that I am virtually stress-free. I recently dislocated my left shoulder and went to my naturopath, who gave me a chiropractic adjustment and popped it back in place. As he was massaging me, he casually commented, "You know, Zig, I don't feel any stress in your body at all." There is none because I know how my life will end, and I know I am the ultimate winner. Each year, I celebrate every birthday because research shows that the more birthdays you have, the longer you will live, so I get excited about that. I never think in terms of being old, but only of getting older, and for many years, I've taken that attitude and approach. My friend and mentor for the last twenty years, Fred Smith, the wisest man I've ever known, frequently asks the question, "Are you living well and will you finish well?" My objective for many years has been to finish well.

Yes, I do believe in working not only hard but smart. Classic example: Most people get about twice as much work done on the day before they go on vacation as they do on an ordinary day. It's not that they know that much more on that particular day, but it's the fact that, in most cases, the night before the day before vacation they list the things they must get done the next day from a sense of responsibility, realizing that the work they leave behind will have to be done by others. The bottom line is that with a game plan—prioritized list of tasks—when they get to work, they do not waste time. They quickly move from one project to the next. In reality—and this is an understatement—the typical employee, in two-minute, four-minute, one-minute, three-minute segments during the day, will totally waste an hour each day of his own time.

But he never stops to talk to himself—he talks to someone else, thereby wasting his time as well.

An hour a day wasted by an individual is five hours a week. That's 250 hours a year and over six weeks of working life. When you take that into consideration, it just means that the people who work consistently are employable at all times, regardless of the economy. And this is especially true if they are constant students.

I am a constant student. I've read an average of over three hours a day for over 30 years, and I read a wide range of materials. I read my Bible every day and the newspaper every day and that way I know what both sides are up to.

I'm a big fan of learning as you go. You can choose whatever you really want and need to learn, and on your way to and from work and around town, you can be learning new things. You can enroll in night classes. You can learn from the Internet. In other words, growth keeps you excited, inspired, and motivated. It prepares you for tomorrow so you can look back on yesterday with a smile. It virtually guarantees your business, personal, and family life will all be better.

I would say that one of the keys in aging smart is the relationships you build over a long period of time. Dr. Dean Ornish of Harvard University, after a 20-year study, came to the conclusion that your relationships have more to do with your physical health than the food you eat, the exercise program you're on, and even the genes you have inherited. Hans Selye, the great stress specialist, says that gratitude is the healthiest of all human emotions. I'm appreciative of the fact that my gratitude bucket regularly overflows with all the good things God sends my way on a regular basis.

Famed psychiatrist Dr. Smiley Blanton also said that in all his years of practice, he had never met even one person, regardless of age, suffering from dementia who practiced these three things:

staying active physically, learning new things, and having a genuine interest in other people.

In my judgment, you get to the goal line of life if you can look into the end zone and examine the relationships you've built, the people you've encouraged, and see many of the things that money will buy and all the things that money won't buy; then you can smile and say, "It's been a good life. I'm glad I was along for the ride."

Life's journey is not to arrive at the grave safely in a well-preserved body, but rather to skid in sideways, totally worn out, shouting, "Holy cow, what a ride!"

PART

III

YOUR SOUL

CHAPTER

7

Nurturing the Soul

Normally, it might be logical to end the book right here. Exercise, eat well, and take care of your mind. These things are important—no, *essential*—to aging well. What more do you need to live smart?

Well, there is something we think gets the short shrift, though it's as equally important in whether you live until you're 99 or collapse at 55.

It's your self, your soul, your inner spirituality.

Let us tell you about a field called psychoneuroimmunology. It's an interesting field because it basically functions like this book—linking separate pieces to compose one whole picture. Psychoneuroimmunologists take a look at things that affect you psychologically, determine how those things get translated physiologically (for example, how does your body interpret a stressful marriage?), and observe the impact on your immune system. An example might be evaluating the chronic stress endured by people who take care of Alzheimer's patients. Remember how we said stress raises the level of inflammation in your body by increasing the number of pro-inflammatory cytokines called Interleukin-6? This high level of chronic inflammation is bad for your immune system; it wears it down. Researchers have found that Alzheimer's caregivers with abnormally high levels of IL-6 in their bodies also have a more difficult time absorbing all the beneficial effects of a flu vaccine. In other words, not only are their immune systems compromised, but they are also not able to benefit from all the effects of a vaccine. The result? They are more susceptible to infectious diseases, vaccines or not. See how it works?

Caregiving Stress ⟶ Inflammation ⟶ Immune System ⟶

Poor Uptake of Flu Vaccine ⟶ Susceptible to Infectious Diseases

Later in this book, we tell you more about the discoveries in this growing field, but psychoneuroimmunologists often look at things such as marriage or religion and their impact on our bodies. They try to provide the link between what's going on in your mind to how that's affecting your body. Their research essentially drives home the point that if you are not happy, not satisfied, or not taking care of yourself emotionally, you're not batting at 1,000. You are racing through life with a leg brace.

Many of us, if we are not feeling right about ourselves, as though something is missing in our lives and we feel unhappy, unsatisfied, or stressed, might turn to a therapist or a best friend or spouse to talk out the feelings. Or we turn to God. Or a book. The result is we miss out on the big picture. We think taking care of ourselves emotionally is just that—taking care of our emotions. We don't think of it in terms of also helping our physical health in *concrete* ways. We don't usually think the way psychoneuroimmunologists do.

One of the first things you need to think about is how to keep yourself happy. How will you live your best life? How will you live well and age well? How will you stay fulfilled? What are the things you can do to make sure you are healthy not only physically but also emotionally and spiritually?

The next few chapters dive deeper into these questions.

■■■ Donald Keough: Forever Coke and Friends

Back in the 1980s and 1990s, Donald Keough was president and chief operating officer for Coca-Cola, one of the most successful brands in the world. He's largely credited with helping build Coke into an American icon and in the process, becoming one of the most admired business leaders.

Don is still on the board of Coca-Cola and despite his many other business positions, from running a New York investment bank, Allen & Co., to sitting on several corporate boards, he's still considered the "Coke man." For a man who ran a business in over 150 countries, you would think he would know a thing or two about maintaining social relationships and how important they are. And you would be correct.

Don sat down and told us why friendships are a rarity in this day and age and why, at nearly 80, he still can't imagine retirement.

There's a great difference between friendship and having a lot of acquaintances. I have a lot of acquaintances because I've done a lot of things in a lot of places. There are moments when you are able to share happy things with people you know from a wide circle of folks that you've touched in your life.

Friendship is a different issue. If you define that word as I define it—as a deep, close relationship where you really know a great deal about each other—I don't think you have many friends of that type. Most of my friendships have developed when I am with people I spend a lot of time with. Warren Buffett and I—by circumstance of life—lived across the street from one another. Neither of us had anything to do. We hadn't conquered anything yet other than we'd gotten married and were beginning to walk through life. And we were able, through a series of years, to touch each other all the time. And now we're both in our seventies, and we've gone through our life together. We know a lot about each other, and we're together often and so it's a great treat.

John White, who worked with me closely all through my presidency and that ended, what, 11 years ago—we still have so much in common. We do a number of things together, and he's a deep friend. We've traveled around the world together. And he knows everything about me—all my faults and all the occasional beauty spots, and vice versa.

Of course, Herbert Allen is a close friend. I met him in September of 1981 when we discussed the possibility of buying Columbia Pictures of which he was chairman. We met at the 21 Club on the second floor and all of a sudden now, that's how many years ago? Over 24 years. He and I have done so many things together. Herb's an intensely interesting person. I tend to enjoy being around people who are conversationalists, who enjoy the stimulation of discussing whatever together. Herb's brilliant at that; so often, our days start in New York over a cup of coffee, and anywhere between 7:15 and 8:30 a.m., we've solved most of the problems of the world.

Some people say they have a hundred friends. I don't know how you can do that. I have a lot of acquaintances that are very dear and very close but that's different than true friendship.

I can tell you that I honestly know a lot more today than I did a year ago. It's because I've been around people and activities in which I've learned and found fascinating. For example, being on Barry Diller's board, which is dealing with the interactive world, we own a dating service. We have roughly a million customers right now who are using the Internet as a way for them to try and locate a person with whom they might have an interest to get to know. As a guy my age, you say that's kind of weird. Well, what was the other way you did it? You went into bars looking for people or you bumped into them in a library or you saw them at church or somewhere. It used to be that when people lived in the same towns, you could find people you could relate to easily. How do you do that in a busy city? How do you do that when you're working eight hours a day?

I'm 78 and still actively involved as executive chairman of Allen & Company, as well as a board member of Coca-Cola and of Berkshire Hathaway, which is a place where age is a benefit and not a detriment. Our vice chairman is over 80. Warren Buffett actively leads at 74. We just brought in Bill Gates to the board, and I think we'll have to pass a resolution to allow younger people to join us because he's just turning 50.

CHAPTER

8

Socialize Your Way to Health

The story goes something like this. In an orphanage in Europe during the 1920s, doctors and nurses were puzzled because they had noticed over the course of several months that every single baby in the nursery cried through the night except one. It wasn't literally only "one" baby. It was one baby in a particular crib, so if the baby changed, the result was still the same. The baby wouldn't cry through the night. The doctors looked hard at why that particular crib always hosted a calm baby.

Later, it was discovered that at the end of every night, the cleaning lady would come into the nursery. The first thing she would do when she entered was cuddle the closest baby to the door. That baby was in the crib that confounded the doctors and nurses. Sadly, with the sheer number of orphaned babies entering the nursery, the doctors and nurses had little time to hold or play with the babies. It was this one brief touch every night that made all the difference for a lucky baby.

That's the power of the human touch, the power of social connections. You need to know, from the moment you are born, that you are not alone.

We can find medicine to help us age better, technology to help us look younger, but there hasn't been a way to duplicate the beneficial effects of social connections. Time and again studies show that social support helps bolster the immune system and helps ward off health problems.

For instance, one study done by Janice Kiecolt-Glaser, a leading researcher in the field of psychoneuroimmunology at Ohio State University, found medical students with better social support than their peers were able to mount a stronger antibody response to a Hepatitis-B vaccine. Another study, also observing medical students (they make easy subjects), discovered lonelier ones had lower natural killer cell activity. Natural killer cells are like soldiers flowing through your blood, blasting away at irregular cell growth that could turn into cancerous tumors. You want lots of these guys swimming through your blood. Other published studies have found spouses of cancer patients, already going through an immense amount of stress, were found to have lower levels of these natural killer cells if they also had lower levels of social support than other spouses of cancer patients.

Have you noticed that you always want your friends and family near you if you are about to deliver a speech or perform on stage for the first time? There's a reason. In one study done at Carnegie Mellon University, researchers found that having just one friend around helps calm a person's blood pressure before performing a nerve-wracking task, such as giving a six-minute speech.

Compelling research has found good social relationships can actually help overcome other health risk factors, such as low socioeconomic status. For reasons that you can imagine, people on the lower rung of the socioeconomic scale are often in poor health. (Money might not buy happiness, but it does protect your health.) These people often carry high *allostatic loads*.

Think of an allostatic load like this: your body, when hit with stresses, has a natural tendency to try to maintain stability. Otherwise, you would never be able to handle stress. Your body tries to get your blood pressure back to normal; it tries to prevent your cholesterol levels from skyrocketing. When cortisol, the stress hormone, is released, the DHEA-S antigen is also released to neutralize the effects. All this creates an *allostatic load*—the evidence left over after your body's been through a struggle. If you have a high allostatic load, you have gone through a lot of stresses; if you have a low allostatic load, you are in better shape. If you carry around a high allostatic load for long periods of time, you are at larger risk for health problems later on, such as cardiovascular disease, diabetes, or even Alzheimer's. Sometimes, researchers refer to allostatic load as a *predisease indicator*.

Carol Ryff, a professor of psychology at the University of Wisconsin-Madison and one of the principal researchers of the Macarthur Mid-Life study, made the fascinating discovery that there are links between social relationships and your allostatic load. She took a sample from the Wisconsin Longitudinal Study— a group of Wisconsin citizens tracked since their high school days in 1957—and found that if a person had positive relationships later on in life, even if that person was born into a family of few means, his or her allostatic load was actually lower than those born into wealth and privilege but who suffered from negative relationships. That is, your socio-economic status, which is a good determinant of health, becomes less important if you have wonderful, positive relationships later on. The key is *later on*. Social connection is not just important at birth. It can make a tremendous difference in your older years. "We see a pattern of resilience that pertains to any period of economic adversity combined with positive relational experience and low allostatic load," Dr. Ryff wrote in her published report on the study.

Betty Liu: The Power of Social Relationships

My father, who is from China, has always had one goal: to come to America to make a better life for his children. In 1976, he passed a medical exam, which gave him entry to practice in the United States. My parents moved here and spent the next 14 years working their way up from job to job to achieve the American middle-class life. They succeeded in sending my sister and me to college. And just when my father could sit back and reap the fruits of his labor, my mother got sick. Very sick. She was diagnosed with lung cancer. After six months, she passed away. That left a huge hole in my father's heart—the person he was going to spend the rest of his life with was gone.

And so for several years, my father was in the very depths of depression. I didn't know it at the time, but looking back, I remember him sitting on the couch on weekends, watching Chinese soap operas from morning until night. Twelve hours straight. There was one night he was boiling a strange mix of celery with some Chinese herbs that smelled like dried fruit stewed in alcohol.

"What is this?" I asked.

"Some Chinese medicine."

"For what?"

"For my blood pressure. The doctor says it's 170 over 110."

I was worried. He was getting sicker every year. He started to walk with a hunch and he wasn't even that old—only 58. He couldn't mow the lawn like he used to and paid the neighborhood boys instead. He was breathless and aging very fast.

When I came back one year from my job overseas, my father looked surprisingly well. He had a bounce in his step. His eyes weren't droopy like they had become. He cooked all day and, in between preparing dishes, told me what had happened.

He decided one day to go back to a boyhood passion. Chinese opera. Before becoming a doctor, my father had wanted to become like those stoic, elegant men trained in the fine art of Peking opera. But he gave that up for the more stable profession of medicine.

So, my father hired an opera teacher to help him with voice lessons. The teacher was from Beijing, my father's hometown. Pretty soon, he and the teacher, Mr. Xao, became friends, and Mr. Xao invited him to a Chinese opera club. My father was surprised they had one in Philadelphia. But sure enough, a club had formed only a year ago for devoted fans of the obscure music genre. In a few weeks, they were all meeting in my father's basement. Every Wednesday night was like my father's version of Poker night—all the guys (and gals) would assemble in his basement to play music, sing, eat, and immerse themselves in opera. My father even began toying with the idea of singing on stage—fulfilling a boyhood dream. But that wasn't the important part. The important part was that he had a social circle. He had friends.

Since then, my father's blood pressure has returned to normal, with the help of medication. At the time of his depression, he couldn't even pick himself up to see the doctor. He feels the singing has helped his lungs—he can breathe better and has more energy. He mows his own lawn now, even though, at 69, I'd rather he didn't. Ever since joining the club, he is more willing to pursue his other passions and open himself to new experiences. He's traveling the world. Three years ago, he opened up his own medical clinic—a goal he has had for decades. Pushing 70, my father says he can't see himself retiring anymore.

It wasn't so clear back then, but my father says the opera club turned his life around. He felt alive around them. The club forced him to turn off the "loner" mentality. That's the power of social relationships. To read about its power is one thing; to see it actually help someone you love is quite something else.

Why are social relationships so powerful? Easy. We circle back again to our dear friend *stress*. Having great social ties, whether it is in your marriage, with your friends, your co-workers, is one of the best ways to alleviate stress. Why do so many American workers, on an average day, gather around the office water cooler? Because aside from the entertainment factor, these small moments of chatting and gossiping about last night's sitcoms are great stress relievers. We naturally seek out these moments.

Robert Kahn, author of *Successful Aging* and professor emeritus of psychology and public health at the University of Michigan, found retirees often say they miss the social network that having a job brought rather than the actual job. "When we ask people who are retiring, or just retired, what they miss most, they seldom say the content of the work itself," he says. "People in the more sophisticated occupations sometimes mention that, but that's because they feel their valued skills and abilities are not being utilized enough. But people coming off the assembly line or the hamburger flipping job do not describe missing the work. They describe missing two things: one is the organization of their time, the sense that they know what's happening day to day. The other is they miss the social relations."

There's probably not a doctor in this world who wouldn't encourage patients to seek comfort with other people. However, here's what you need to remember. You will have to work a little harder at making social connections as you age. Think of it in the same way as exercise. Everyone needs to exercise, but as you age, it becomes increasingly necessary. The same goes for social relationships. However, this is *just* at the time when it becomes *more difficult* to get on the treadmill or to stay socially connected. Friends don't come as easy when we get older. When you retire, you will not go to an office anymore and you are not meeting new people every day. Or you might have, sadly, seen your spouse—your biggest source of support—succumb to cancer or another disease.

Sociologists have, from time to time, discussed a "structural lag" when it comes to understanding why it's harder for us stay socially connected into old agedom. As Dr. Linda Fried, the director of the Center on Aging and Health at the Johns Hopkins University School of Medicine wrote, "Although evidence is mounting that remaining active and engaged is beneficial as one ages, our society has not developed approaches that support such activity for the broad spectrum of adults."

A Case in Point: Working in the Schools of Baltimore

Back in 1999, a group of researchers, led by Dr. Linda Fried at the Johns Hopkins University School of Medicine, decided to experiment with one solution to this "structural lag," where social institutions appear to be lagging behind the needs of an aging population. They helped develop a program called Experience Corps (www.experiencecorps.org), which put older adults from 60 and up into volunteer positions at elementary schools around the country. Dr. Fried studied the program in Baltimore. The major feature was the program required real involvement with the kids—this wasn't merely babysitting. The volunteers committed 15 hours a week over a full school year in programs to enhance literacy or problem-solving skills. Most of the volunteers were African American women who signed up because they wanted to make a difference.

The researchers were heartened by the results. After a year of volunteering, the adults were healthier, and 63 percent said they were more active than they had been previously. For instance, the number of blocks walked increased 31 percent. The use of canes fell. Television watching—a huge pastime among older adults—dropped 4 percent. A bonus was that social relationships developed. A large number of the volunteers said they had a bigger circle of friends to turn to for help, such as checking in on them if they became ill.

Even better news was that 82 percent of the volunteers said they would stay in the program for another year or longer. Since then, the program has been expanded to several more American cities and involves more than 1,000 volunteers. It may not be exactly the kind of activity you are looking for, but it's a start in the right direction.

Think about it. As children, we have school, which is teeming with people and activities. Then, we start our careers and immediately meet new people every day. We build strong friendships. Staying socially connected throughout much of our lives is almost effortless. Then, as we hit our 50s and 60s, when we begin to envision retirement, we see that the number of people we interact with every day will suddenly shrink from dozens to maybe three or four. Or even just one—our spouse.

What are the options? Join a bowling league? The church? If those options don't appeal to you, you are not alone. There aren't enough choices out there to replicate the social exhilaration we felt throughout much of our lives. The best thing to do is to plan ahead for your later years. Make sure you have done enough to ensure not only a financially secure future, but also a vibrant and social one. It may be launching a second career as we discuss in Chapter 13, "Get Out of the Dilbert Syndrome: When a Second Career Just Might Be the Answer." Or it may be diving into a hobby. You may even want to embark on some serious volunteer work.

No one can tell you how to gain friends or have a happy marriage. It's like telling someone how to find his or her true love. That doesn't work. The important thing is that you realize how important relationships are to your survival. Treasure your friends. Respect your wife or husband. He or she might drive you nuts from time to time, but you are better off with them than without them.

To Be or Not to Be. . .Wed? How Marriage Adds or Subtracts Years from Your Life

If you are a husband, buy roses for your wife tonight. Massage her feet. Give her a backrub. Your longevity might depend on it!

Turns out, marriage can add years to a man's life. Recently, an increasing amount of research has shown that the deep social connection a marriage creates enhances a man's health and, therefore, his longevity. Dr. Michael Roizen, who wrote *Real Age* in 1999, estimates a good marriage may add 1.5 years to a man's life and half a year to a woman's life. Another study of 3,000 elderly men and women in Australia found that married men lived about a year longer than single ones.

Dr. Janice Kiecolt-Glaser of Ohio State University, who has conducted several marriage studies, says men benefit the most from a marriage because "they tend not to have social networks. If a man is married, at least he has one close social contact."

Women, she notes, are different, and "they have a much broader, diverse network of contacts." This might explain why they get a smaller boost, if any, from a good marriage. According to Dr. Roizen's calculations, single women experience no change in lifespan, whereas single men can expect their lives to be three years shorter than married men.

Researchers say part of the reason might be that women, in general, are more sensitive to the ups and downs in a marriage, just as they are to stresses in everyday life. As Dr. Kiecolt-Glaser has observed dozens of married couples in her lab, she has noticed that the wives tend to have a more difficult time returning the levels of cortisol and other stress hormones to "normal" after a heated argument. And when asked to recount a recent negative event, Dr. Kiecolt-Glaser found women tend to be more accurate in their description than men. Apparently, when it comes to marriage problems, men tend to better deal with the stresses by just letting them wash away. "Men just don't see negative events and hostility in quite the same way as women," Dr. Kiecolt-Glaser says.

The operative word in all this, of course, is "happy." No man (or woman) will live longer if stuck in an unhappy union. Far be it for us to advise you on how to make a marriage work. Our only advice would be to evaluate it as if your life depended on it!

▪▪▪ Andrew Young: Statesman, Civil Rights Leader

Money doesn't buy happiness, but as we discussed earlier, it certainly does buy you some assurance of good health. Of course, if you have unhealthy social relationships or become overweight and lazy, you say goodbye to those benefits of wealth.

What happens, though, to those people who have experienced traumatic events and still manage to live long, healthy lives? The Holocaust survivors. The World War II veterans. Of course, people sometimes do not survive these kinds of experiences emotionally intact—if they survive at all. For those who do, however, they are often in touch with something inside themselves that helps guide them through a long life. The Civil Rights movement in the South was a gut-wrenching time for this country. For those black Americans who were on the ground organizing protests, recruiting volunteers, and dodging death threats, it was an era that left many battle wounds, both physical and mental.

Andrew Young, a minister by training, was by Martin Luther King's side throughout much of the movement, and in the process, he had a front seat into both the beauty and ugliness that was America in the 1960s. As it turned out, that seat made Andrew Young an eyewitness to history on that fateful day in April 4, 1968, when Dr. King was assassinated in Memphis, Tennessee. The death of his friend and mentor became one of several life-altering moments in Andrew Young's life, propelling him to a career of public service.

Many of us will thankfully never go through such times, even though it is in these moments that we often become intimate with our *soul*. The lesson in Andrew's story is that he took those pivotal moments in life and built upon them, fulfilling what he saw as a "higher calling." He later became mayor of Atlanta and then an ambassador to the United Nations. Today, he continues his work through Goodworks International.

He recently sat down with us and discussed how his tremendous life experiences have shaped his views on aging.

I come from a family of fairly long livers. I always said that Jesus didn't figure out who he was until 30. And that St. Augustine didn't even get converted until he was 35. Albert Schweitzer was 55 when his life began to come together. I always figured I had until 55 before I decided what I wanted to do with my life.

I keep working at 73 because I have a clear purpose that almost nobody else sees. I always say that life begins at 40, and that 40 to 50 is spring training. You don't really know—you don't really begin to get enough confidence to make happen what you really have come to know until you've played around with it a lot for ten years. Usually, by the time you're 50, you're pretty certain.

I think the first book that I read that made me think about changing the world without violence was a little book that Nehru did on Gandhi. In fact, that's the title of it, Nehru on Gandhi.

Martin Luther King, Jr. never thought he was doing enough. He always felt that his own life was undisciplined, and while he would never admit it—well, he wouldn't call it fear and I don't think it was fear—he knew that any decision he made would probably lead to his death. He was very careful and cautious about the decisions he made. He didn't make a decision unless it was something he felt was worthy of risking his life. He got stabbed, you see, when he was 27. In Harlem, this crazy woman just came up and stuck a letter opener in his chest. He used to joke about that. He said, "Well, if you gotta get stabbed, there's no better place to get stabbed than in Harlem."

I played tennis and I rode my bicycle until a couple of years ago. Then I had a combination of prostate cancer and a busted knee, and I had to give up both of those. So now, really all I do is swim. I was a swimmer in college. I swim just about as well as I did then. You don't lose it. For my 72nd birthday, I decided I was going to swim 72 laps in an hour, and I did it in 54 minutes to raise money for the Y.

Everything that has ever happened in my life happened after everything I planned for failed. When MLK went to jail in Birmingham, it was because everybody said we failed. He said, "I can't go around and leave these kids. I, in good faith, asked these young people to go to jail and the only thing I can do is go with them."

That was the weekend that the clergy wrote a letter to the press condemning him for all of this; and he was furious, in jail, in solitary confinement. That's when he started writing the letter from the Birmingham jail around the margins of the newspaper, on toilet paper, anything he could write on.

It changed everything for me.

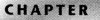

CHAPTER

Having Purpose

In the last chapter, you considered how staying socially connected can do wonders for your health as you age. Now, you will look inward.

Anyone who spends enough time reflecting on his or her life will start to wonder, "What is my purpose in life?"

Is it to be the best salesperson in your company? Is it to be a good Christian? Is it to cure cancer?

There are some peak occurrences when this question is particularly relevant, like late adolescence or the period after a job loss or the birth of a new baby. In great moments in our lives, this is the question that confronts us all.

We can't emphasize enough how healthy this is. Time and again, patients who search for meaning and purpose in their lives after a major illness tend to have lower mortality and morbidity rates. For instance, heart attack patients who altered their philosophies on life and their values after the attack—even seeing the episode as a benefit—were less likely to experience another attack, even eight years down the road, according to a 1987 study published in the *Journal of Consulting & Clinical Psychology*. A more recent study by researchers at UCLA found that women who had lost a close relative to breast cancer had higher levels of natural killer cell cytotoxicity if they also placed greater importance on "goals such as cultivating relationships, personal development, and striving for meaning in life."

Researchers are just beginning to understand the true power of purpose, and here are a few theories:

- **Purpose gives people a greater sense of control**. "What is my purpose?" is another way of saying "What can I do in my life that's meaningful?" A person who sees great purpose in his or her life is also in control of it. Control becomes increasingly important to our mental and physical health as we age.

- **Purpose enhances the right behaviors.** For reasons that may seem obvious, people who have meaning and purpose in their lives tend to make better behavior choices. They are not binge drinkers. They exercise. They keep their weight down. They enjoy life, so they do things that will prolong life, not destroy it.

- **Purpose is driven by and promotes cognitive function.** It takes a great deal of mental energy to find our purpose, and anything that requires us to use our brains to the maximum is good for our bodies (see Part II, "Your Mind"). No lazy mind will ever lead us to purpose and meaning. Deep thinking equals a healthier you.

Our friend and mentor, Tom Johnson, is the former top guy at CNN, the Cable News Network. He was one of the masterminds behind the network's landmark Gulf War reporting in 1990-91 and organized coverage of other historic world events in his 11-year run as CEO of the various CNN cable networks. Prior to that, Tom was the publisher of *The Los Angeles Times*—typical Type-A news guy.

About four years ago, Tom was feeling burned out. He was, in his words, getting frustrated with the red tape at CNN. "I was tired of always having somebody above me pulling my chain," he said. He went back and forth on whether to retire, scribbling notes to himself on any writing surface nearby, from dinner napkins to the cardboard covers of his drycleaning hangers. After a few months of restless nights and a drawer full of lists, Tom, at age 59, decided to hang up his hat and leave the daily grind of broadcast news.

Shortly after his retirement, Tom wrote the foreword to a memoir by J.B. Fuqua, the multimillionaire businessman known for his philanthropy, who revealed in his book his struggles with clinical depression. Coincidentally, Tom suffered from depression through much of his life, and after retirement, he has been working to help others cope with the illness. He's spoken frankly about his thoughts of suicide to help people confront the disease. Tom told us that his informal campaign to fight depression and help those who suffer from it was a way of "giving back." He says he's happier now than he's been in a long time. "If I'd known retirement would be like this, I'd have done it sooner!" he jokes.

J.B. Fuqua: Businessman Turned Philanthropist

John Brooks "J.B." Fuqua, now 87, epitomizes the true "rags to riches" story in America, having made himself a multimillionaire from nothing.

Despite his success as a businessman, J.B. is best known for giving away his money to good causes, something plenty of rich people talk about but rarely do. He's given away $160 million of his personal fortune and pledges $10 million a year to a number of groups. He famously endowed Duke University's business school as repayment for all those years the college library lent him books to read. As a teenager, J.B. was too poor to afford college.

J.B. also broke the silence on depression among business executives when he revealed his troubles with the lifelong illness. He shared his experience with mental depression in a memoir published in 2001. His memoir sparked a public discussion in the media about the prevalence of clinical depression. As J.B. can attest, giving back in several ways can offer you a great deal of purpose.

So many people just keep accumulating money and they really don't have any objective as to what they're going to do about it. If you ask them about it, they say, "I'm gonna leave it to my children." Well, that's good for the children sometimes, but it's really not a good use for the money, at least not for all of it.

The idea is to save and to invest, not to try to get rich quick. Relate the amount you save at various times in your life to your expected cost of living during your retirement. However, after you calculate your expected spending during retirement, save a surplus well beyond that. You need this surplus for the unexpected expenses that surely will arise, especially for healthcare.

Certainly, one of the major reasons for people not really getting anywhere in their career is because they don't have the courage to do things. Risk is related to reward. If people learn how to take substantial risk intelligently, they are usually successfully rewarded for that. The most important thing is having the courage to go ahead and do what you think you can do, and to prepare for that transition period when your income might be less than it has been.

I've always been an optimist. If I ever employ somebody or if I'm gonna make friends with them, I want them to be an optimist because if they're not an optimist, they can't perform in anything very well. You have to be with people who are optimistic and people who also have courage.

Whether you get to be a happy, whole person will be largely determined by your sense of curiosity. If you want to learn something and you read all the time and expect to learn something new, you're certainly better off than if you don't have curiosity. In my case, I contend that I have as much curiosity as I had when I was 18 and 20 years old. And I'm proud of it. It certainly had a great deal to do with my career. It has to do with my happiness now.

Every year Forbes magazine has an issue where they select the 400 wealthiest people in the country. It's interesting to go through that list and see that most of them did not inherit their wealth. And so that proves to me that you can get rich in this country without inheriting it, and you can get rich without having many things that would appear to give you opportunities to get rich. I don't think I've ever made a dishonest nickel in my life. It's very important that people realize that they don't have to do dishonest things in order to make a fortune. You find that just the opposite is true. Most people who have become wealthy are very honest, and that's one of the reasons that they are so successful.

That's lesson number one in how to find purpose. Give something back. It's as easy as that. You hear that phrase all the time. "I want to give something back to my community." People, as they get older, have an intrinsic need to help others when they achieve a certain stature or wealth. Some people do it for the wrong reasons (such as they want some glory or their name plastered all over the side of a building). However, most of the time, people genuinely feel an urge to do something for someone else, with no expectations of a return.

We say don't wait until you retire or accumulate a certain amount of wealth to give back. Do it now. It might be volunteering once or twice a month at your local store or giving horseback riding lessons to underprivileged children, or mentoring a young intern at your company. The point is to do something for someone else, without expecting anything back in return. There are probably a dozen nonprofit organizations in your city dying to have you and your expertise, but unable to pay for it. Do it for free. Commit to giving back.

Giving back goes hand in hand with having a sense of purpose. You will make your community a much better place and help yourself in the process.

A second way to find purpose is to believe in something. Because almost 94 percent of Americans say they believe in God, it is logical for us to discuss the role of religion in finding and having purpose. There's a reason why one of the bestselling books over the past several years happens to be based on the Bible and titled, *The Purpose-Driven Life*. For many Americans, purpose is inexorably linked with believing in God.

Whatever floats your boat. Regardless of whether you believe in God, Allah, or the Laughing Buddha, the important thing is that as you age, you need to keep believing in something.

Many doctors are uncomfortable about bringing religion into their patients' treatment programs. Most of the time, they don't unless the patient mentions his or her own faith. However, that doesn't stop the medical community from researching the benefits of believing in God.

Studies have shown that religious people tend to cope better with stress, live longer, and develop fewer chronic diseases. One University of Iowa study published in 2004 sampled 557 older adults and found that those who regularly attended church had lower levels of, you guessed it, those nasty Interleukin-6 cytokines. It doesn't appear to take much to attain those lower cytokine levels—amazingly, going to church once or twice a week is enough to bring these levels down.

Here's further food for thought: Another study examined religious attendance among Mexican Americans and found that those who attended church even once a week saw their risk of mortality reduced by 32 percent compared to those who never attended—32 percent! That's a big drop for a once-a-week commitment.

Is God helping us live longer? That's certainly beyond the scope of *anyone's* knowledge. But it's safe to say that believing in something—a higher being, a spiritual philosophy, a set of morals—tends to help people live longer and healthier. In general, religious people are more likely not to smoke and lead clean, less risky lifestyles; they value family and are involved in society (all important factors for good health and longevity).

Religion also adds another element not often thought of: It gives people a sense of control. "I'll leave my fate in God's hands," is a common refrain for religious people when faced with difficulties in their lives, say a death of a loved one or the onset of a chronic illness. Ironically, by ceding control to "God" or one's faith, this gives people a *greater* feeling of control. Oftentimes, what matters is not so much that you can control the outcome of these trying times (because you can't), but that you are controlling your attitude and behavior.

Of course, when it comes to events where you can exert great influence, it does matter that you can control the result. A study of elderly people who had some control over which nursing home to live in were found to have lower stress levels than those with no choice. One study found that when subjects were able to master control over some new and difficult tasks, their levels of catecholamine fell. Catecholamines are chemical substances in your body tuned into your "fight or flight" responses in times of stress. They cause your blood pressure to rise and your heart rate to jump. You don't need to be a control freak, but it's easy to see how having a say in your life—or at least feeling your life is not out of your hands—can improve your quality of life as you age.

This brings us to our third and last thought: Remember that having purpose is one of the ways to achieve happiness.

Let's first discuss a little about happiness. Over the last several decades, the field of psychology has been particularly interested in the idea of figuring out what makes human beings happy.

Maybe it's because we are such a materially rich nation, yet it's become even clearer that money does not buy happiness. So what does?

Inevitably, the idea of happiness boils down to two perspectives with two names that sound like mythical Greek creatures. One is called *hedonia* and means you are happy if you feel happy. Think Bobby McFerrin's "Don't worry, be happy" ditty. The other is called *eudaimonia* and means you are happy if you are, such as the U.S. Army slogan, "be all that you can be." If you are growing personally, you are achieving your dreams, you are in control of your environment, and you are pursuing a purposeful life, then you are "happy."

Happy Brain = Better Health?

If we are happy people, do our brains act differently? Research says, so far, yes.

Richard Davidson, a leading neuroscientist at the University of Wisconsin-Madison, has produced a wealth of data that shows people with unusually more activity in the left front part of the brain are generally happier people. However, does this have anything to do with our health?

Possibly. Dr. Davidson has spent decades reading brain waves and brain activity—even those of the Dalai Lama and his monks—and the link to natural killer cells (yes, those little soldiers again). What Dr. Davidson found is that more activity in the left prefrontal area of the brain correlates with higher levels of natural killer cells. In one study of psychology students, Dr. Davidson observed their brain waves and natural killer cell activity over an academic year. During their most stressful exam time periods, Dr. Davidson found left-brained students—the generally happier ones—had a higher level of natural killer cell activity than the right-brained ones. He also showed the students some happy and sad film clips from movies like The *Lady and the Tramp*, *Parenthood*, and *Beaches*, and he discovered right-brained students had a much lower increase in natural killer cell activity during the happy film moments than their left-brained counterparts.

It's not clear why this area of the brain affects natural killer cells, but at least you know happiness pays off in more ways than one.

People, as they grow older and enter the post-retirement phase, do not naturally become less happy. However, they do suffer from some loss of personal growth, as Dr. Ryff, the University of Wisconsin psychology professor whose research you read about earlier, found. They lose their place in society because their career has ended. They lose a little control over their environment—maybe the thoughts of disease and aching bones loom large. They are, in other words, less happy in the eudaimonic sense.

"Many older people are actually having some difficulties, some challenges in finding ways to remain purposefully and meaningfully engaged," she told us. "They need to find ways to utilize their talents and abilities in order to make a contribution."

Your goal as you age is to keep that eudaimonic gas tank filled. You do that in part by making sure you continue to have a purpose. You explore your options of giving back. You pursue new careers and hobbies. You continue to develop social connections. You consider all this later, but essentially, keep in mind that having purpose is good for society and good for you. It's important. Make sure you don't sell your happiness short as you age. Think of all the people we interviewed for this book— the role models. All of them are at an advanced age and doing the things they do because even though they widely vary in how well they eat, how much exercise they do, how active they stay, they are all the same in one regard: They continue to lead purposeful and meaningful lives.

■■■ Satisfaction with Life Scale

Are you satisfied?

Well, here's an easy one-minute way to find out. Ed Diener is a psychologist at the University of Illinois and a leading thinker on the subject of happiness—the hedonic kind. He developed a short questionnaire that he shares with the public to determine your life satisfaction. If you want to learn more about happiness, you can check out the doctor's website at www.psych. uiuc.edu/~ediener.

Following are five statements with which you may agree or disagree. Using the 1–7 scale below, indicate your agreement with each item by placing the appropriate number beside that item. Then add up your total to see how satisfied you are with your life. Please be open and honest in your responses.

7	Strongly agree
6	Agree
5	Slightly agree
4	Do not agree or disagree
3	Slightly disagree
2	Disagree
1	Strongly disagree

In most ways, my life is close to my ideal. _____

The conditions of my life are excellent. _____

I am satisfied with my life. _____

So far, I have gotten the important things I want in life. _____

If I could live my life over, I would change almost nothing. _____

Results:

35 – 31 Extremely satisfied

26 – 30 Satisfied

21 – 25 Slightly satisfied

20 Neutral

15 – 19 Slightly dissatisfied

10 – 14 Dissatisfied

5 – 9 Extremely dissatisfied

▰▰ Rosalynn Carter: Former First Lady on Life's Purpose

Rosalynn Carter is often known as the former first lady whose quiet presence by Jimmy Carter's side helped him ascend to the presidency of the United States. But she has also, on her own, become one of the nation's leading advocates for mental health. During her husband's tenure in the White House, Rosalynn focused on overhauling the mental healthcare system and became the honorary chair of the President's Commission on Mental Health.

She continues her work today through the Carter Center. Every year, she hosts the Rosalynn Carter Symposium on Mental Health Policy, drawing in top leaders and policy thinkers from various fields to address the many problems in our mental healthcare system. Rosalynn Carter's work on mental health reflects her passion for helping those who are disadvantaged and making sure the issues involved aren't swept under the rug.

Rosalynn Carter is fast approaching 80, but like her husband, she is still busy and active. She attributes her long life to her strong marriage to Jimmy Carter. Both have become accomplished people by pursuing interests together—and separately.

When we interviewed Jimmy Carter, he told us that his strong marriage to Rosalynn was instrumental in helping him age well. However, he also told us something else that was revealing—that both he and Rosalynn agreed early on to give each other "space." In some ways, having separate pursuits was as important to their marriage as having joint interests. This "separate, but together" philosophy is vitally important for any marriage—or union—to work.

Being active and having a mission has been very important to me. My work as an advocate for mental health has helped keep me vigorous and active for the past 35 years. I have worked on promoting mental health and trying to help those with mental illness since 1971, when Jimmy became governor. It has given me my own mission.

When I began, I saw the huge need for someone to work to help both people suffering from mental illness and their families. Back then, people with mental illness were usually just sedated and kept out of sight. There was a huge stigma associated with mental illness. Compared to physical illnesses, mental illnesses received very low funding. It was not fair, and so much could be done to alleviate suffering and promote wellness. It is really fulfilling to me to continue to make a difference.

After you meet people with mental illness, you see how much they need help. The families also often need help. Most families are touched by it one way or another, so it is an issue where proper education and treatment can do so much good.

My own work, my mission to promote mental health, has given me a real purpose that is important to me. I have no doubt that keeping such a real purpose and keeping so busy has helped me age well. I don't even think about getting old—I'm too busy!

Jimmy always says, "Try to do something that you don't think you can do, as it will give you self-esteem when you find you are able to do it." I learned to ski at 59 years old! That was something I thought I could never do.

I grew up in the Bible Belt. I grew up in the church. I am a Christian, and it has always been a part of my life. I don't ever remember a time when I did not believe in Jesus and go to Sunday school and church.

You asked if I fall back on one thing in times of stress. Once, there was a Billy Graham crusade that came to Plains, Georgia back in the days of segregation. Jimmy was in charge of organizing it. He had it in a movie theatre (because churches were segregated and would not accept an integrated audience).

It was so important to us to have black and white people working together, which was just about unheard of in those times.

They taught us to say as we walked down the aisle, "I can do all things through Christ, whose strength is in me." I have been in all kinds of situations in my life when I had no idea whether I could do it, and I just turn to that Bible verse. It helps when you think you just cannot do something.

I'd like to offer everyone two concluding thoughts I hope people find valuable. I'm a workaholic by nature and love to keep busy helping others each day, but balance is important. Jimmy has always insisted that you take some time out every day. Do something you like, such as exercise, perhaps ride bikes, but get away from your work each day.

Finally, it is important for older people to do an oral history of their lives. A younger relative can have a conversation with you, asking you questions and casually recording it. Everyone is important and should feel that way. People will want to hear your story. It will mean so much to your family. I wish my mother had done it.

YOUR MONEY
AND YOUR JOB

Don't Let the Money Control You: Saving Smart for Lifelong Security and Success

Let's face it; most of us find dealing with personal finances a pain.

Unless you're making millions of dollars like the head of a huge multinational company and don't need to worry about exhausting your money tree, chances are you're concerned about making your money last throughout your older years.

Even if you fall into the upper middle class, you're still likely concerned and thinking about how you will maintain your lifestyle if you stop working past 65. You probably don't expect or want to suddenly downgrade your quality of life after you reach a certain age. So, you should plan to make sure you can, at the very least, remain at the level of living that you've become accustomed.

Money is quite often one of the single biggest sources of stress in life. The other, which is discussed in the next section, is work. Marriages often break up over disagreements about finances, either because one partner is too careless with the cash or the other is too selfish. Money, or the lack thereof, is a great destabilizer in people's lives. Money can often control people because they don't know how to control it.

It's ridiculous to discuss aging well without touching upon finances. As mentioned in previous chapters, there's no doubt wealthier people tend to have a greater chance for healthier lives. Money is a great determinant of health. Consider that those living in the poorest parts of the United States often possess the highest mortality rates.

Yet time and again you have probably heard the same old thing: Americans are frighteningly unprepared for retirement. As a society, Americans live on borrowed money too much, piling up debt to live beyond their means. Some do not know how to invest in the stock or bond markets. Many are living paycheck to paycheck.

Taking control of your aging means you unequivocally must take control of your money. Only then—and this is important—can you *truly* plan for the future.

Several excellent books can help you learn more about investing. To understand why it is so hard to pick individual stocks and beat the market, read Burton Malkiel's classic *Random Walk Down Wall Street*. To understand why stocks in general are necessary as part of your overall wealth portfolio, read Jeremy J. Siegel's *Stocks for the Long Run*. Another book, *The Millionaire Next Door*, takes a great look at why saving is so important for your financial future. *The Millionaire Next Door* makes the useful point that it is how much you save, and how well you avoid debt, and not just your earned income that can help you become a secure millionaire. In light of this, the focus of this chapter is how to save early, continuously, and smart.

It is also well worth your time to sit down with a financial planner, even if it is only for a free consultation (American Express, for instance, offers free sessions for card members). You don't have to hire this person, unless of course you like him. You might not be able to afford his services just yet. The point is that you need to start taking steps (even small steps) that will reinforce the point that you are taking control of your money.

When dealing with personal finances, it can seem as if too much information and conflicting advice is out there. Throw in personal fears and aversion to or tolerance for risk and no wonder many people remain paralyzed when planning for retirement. If this applies to you, know that you are not alone. Even financial planners fail in dealing with their own financial futures. Take heart that everyone has a difficult time dealing with their own personal finances because they are just that—personal.

This section of the book aims to filter out the noise and outline a clear strategy for thinking about your finances. Remember that your objective is not to become the savviest stock picker on Main Street, but to simply organize your finances so that you are intelligently well prepared and positioned for your future. It doesn't matter that the next guy says he made millions investing in something like Google stock; what matters is that even when the stock markets go bust or the bond markets tank, you've got some clear tools and strategies to help you face the future confidently while everyone else scrambles to cover their losses.

▪▪▪ It Always Begins with Saving

Our first strategy is a maddeningly simple one: save, save, save.

Why maddeningly? Because if everyone followed this advice, no one would have to worry so much about retirement.

Americans have one of the worst savings rates in the world. Many Americans live on credit because they have saved so little, whereas Asians sit on piles of cash. In many Asian countries, savings rates reach 30 percent of incomes. Amazingly, and perhaps to an extreme, savings rates in China have risen to 50 percent. Picture the future leadership in the global economy if Chinese save and invest and Americans continue to borrow and spend!

A large part of the relatively high savings in Asia has to do with the fact that many Asian countries still do not have mature credit markets or credit-rating agencies, so people find it difficult to borrow money.

For those readers who have not yet started a steady and adequate saving strategy, don't feel guilty about not saving. However, do realize that one absolutely crucial element to financial freedom is to save a substantial portion of your income and to start saving early. Numerous studies support the idea that it is your *saving behavior*—even more than your skill or luck at picking investments—that ultimately is the main driver of your wealth accumulation.

It is important for you to save early, significantly, and consistently throughout your working life. A rough rule of thumb is to save about 20 percent of your income, even if your income is low. This is just a rough rule because you may have to save more to "catch up" if you start to save rather late in your working life. As one example, later in this chapter, we present a savings scheme by the Schwab Center for Investment Research that is tailored for people in specific age brackets. We offer no explicit endorsements, but the scheme is clear. A strict savings rule may not be easy, but the point is to adjust your lifestyle expectations. Control your spending behavior, if needed.

Twenty percent of your income may sound steep. Consider, however, that the definition of savings, at least according to economists, is all the income you put away instead of consuming. This is not just money put into your bank account but also added to your stock and bond portfolios, IRA, 401(k), and any other investment vehicles. Note the difference in this definition of savings versus the more colloquial usage of "my savings"; that is, "my total money in the bank." Total money in bank accounts and similar deposits are regarded as part of the asset class termed "cash" in your overall investment portfolio. Savings, on the other hand, are considered *added flows* into your investment portfolio, which then get allocated into different asset categories, such as stocks or bonds or simply cash.

The earlier you start saving, the more you'll benefit from the joys of compound interest or compounded returns on your investments. If you start early, you have a lot of time left for your investments to earn interest on the prior interest you continuously earn, as well as on the amount you save and invest. Due to compounding, your wealth doesn't grow in a straight line, it grows *exponentially*.

The Joy of Compounding

Jeff, being born before the age of ubiquitous computers, remembers the joys of compound interest from his trips to the local bank as a youngster. At the bank, the interest credited to his account would be stamped right into the savings account passbook.

Jeff started with $100. His bank gave 4 percent annual interest, compounded quarterly. At 1 percent per quarter, he saw $101 in his account after the first quarter. Three months later, he was so excited when he noticed his total jumped to $102.01, not just $102. He earned $0.01 in extra interest due to compounding. Sure, it was only a penny so far, but this "interest on the prior interest" would grow and pick up steam later.

An economist (some would say a geek) was born!

The following figure illustrates the concept that savings invested early do not just grow at a straight line or linear rate, but at an accelerating or *exponential* rate. Starting your saving early will lead to a dramatically higher amount of wealth when you reach more senior ages. The results are so significant that learning and applying the lesson of saving early can indeed dramatically boost your financial freedom and security in later life.

The graph shows the amount of pre-tax money you will have at age 70 in a tax-deferred account if you save $10,000 at various age points. Saving a solid sum starting even as late as 60 can make a big difference by age 70, and, of course, even more so if you keep it invested beyond age 70, especially if you stay invested aggressively and achieve an 8 percent average annual return.

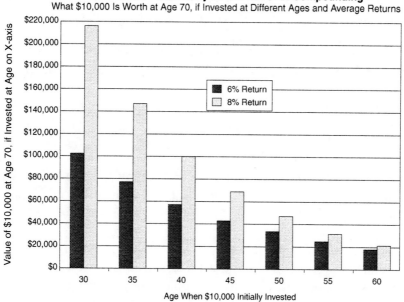

Save Smart—Start Early for the Power of Compounding
What $10,000 Is Worth at Age 70, if Invested at Different Ages and Average Returns

The figure also illustrates the impact of going for a portfolio of 8 percent average returns versus a more conservative one of 6 percent average annual gains. Obviously, if you can create an investment portfolio that has a good chance of giving you higher returns, it makes a big difference. However, the main point illustrated is the importance of starting as early as you can. Even if you feel it is too late, don't worry. The important thing is to *start now.*

The power of compounding is shown by the two "start at age 30" bars. At 6 percent annual returns, you would have a very respectable sum of over $100,000 at age 70 on your $10,000 initial investment. So, the first key is to start as early as you can.

The second key is to invest boldly enough to gain those extra percentage points of growth over time. You can see how just a few percentage points of return can make a big difference. Starting at age 30, if you can achieve 8 percent annual returns on average, you will have a whopping $217,245 by 70. This large sum is nearly 22 times the money you put in and more than twice the total if you earned a 6 percent return on average.

How do you get such a wonderfully multiplied sum from a modest initial investment? A handy rule used by financial professionals is the "rule of 72." It is a simple mathematical equation, as follows:

72/% Rate of Return = Number of Years for Money to Double

This tells you approximately how many years it will take for your money to double if you earn a certain percentage rate of return.

For example, if you earn a 4 percent return in a bank certificate of deposit (CD) or a U.S. Treasury note or bond, you must wait almost 18 years to see your money double (72 divided by 4 is 18). At 6 percent, you reduce the doubling period to 12 years (72 divided by 6 is 12). Eight percent gets exciting as you double your money every 9 years. Naturally, 9 percent average returns, compounded continuously, mean you can double your investment in merely 8 years.

The key to compounding at constant growth rates is that it leads to exponential, not linear or straight-line, growth. Take a look at the following figure, which shows the exponential growth path of a $10,000 investment. Note in particular the sharp upturn associated with the 8 percent return.

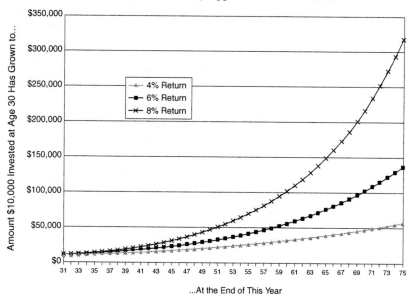

Invest Smart—Stay Aggressive but Diversified

The good news is that it is never too late to start saving, just like it is never too late to reap substantial benefits by starting the right exercise program (see Part I, "Your Body"). It is better to save aggressively in your 50s and even 60s than to try to live on only a small Social Security check after you retire.

If you start saving late, you *must* save a greater proportion of your income. This is logical because you must make up for lost time and lost longer-term compounding benefits. The Schwab Center for Investment Research has some excellent guidelines on how much of your income you should save as you age.

If you start saving steadily while still in your 20s (bravo for you!), you can usually save only 10 to 15 percent of your income. This should be enough to generate a substantial nest egg for you if maintained throughout your career.

If you wait until your 30s before you start saving, you are like many average Americans, so you need to consistently save between 15 and 25 percent of your income.

If you wait until your 40s, you need to save between 25 and 35 percent of your income. Sure this sounds steep, but you have to make up for lost time accumulating wealth.

Clearly, people in their 50s and 60s who have not saved are behind the curve. However, don't get depressed. Just know that it is never too late to start. If possible, save 30 percent and, ideally, an even greater proportion of your income. If this is not possible, do what you can to stay in mental and physical shape because you will likely need to continue working for a while. Follow the advice earlier in this book: Find some work you love and you won't dread your later years. Indeed, the work may keep you active, productive, and feeling great about those later years.

Growing Your Wealth: Investing Well

Now that you have begun to accumulate your savings steadily, what do you do with it?

After you have some money, your goal is to preserve the capital while earning a good rate of return. One way to lose all your money is to try any number of "get rich quick" schemes, including investing in the next hot stock you see hyped on TV or in an unsolicited e-mail. You can get rich slowly if you save enough consistently and invest it for solid, if unspectacular, rates of return.

The key to minimizing risk is *diversification*. You can try your hand at riskier investments, but only if your entire portfolio is balanced and diversified. That could mean having some high-risk along with some low-risk investments. The key is that your combined assets, your eggs, are put in enough different baskets that your overall profile has much less risk than if you had not diversified.

In this case, having high-risk assets does not mean buying the next speculative stock you hear about. Instead, it refers to putting money into areas with a potentially higher rate of return, such as emerging markets. A classic law of finance is that assets that on average yield higher returns do this to compensate for higher risk.

We discuss this in more detail and explain what elements ought to make up your portfolio, but first, a little about diversification.

When investing, the ideal situation is to follow this maxim: buy low, sell high. The other basic law of finance is to diversify your wealth. Spread your investments in a portfolio of different asset classes. Essentially, don't put all your eggs in one basket. Don't be like those unfortunate Worldcom or Enron employees who, in addition to losing their jobs and income, lost their wealth because they invested most of their money in their own company's stock. Don't put both your job and your wealth in the hands of a single company, no matter how loyal you are to it.

Why does diversifying protect your downside? The obvious reason is that when some assets suffer big price declines, others may not. When stocks go down, other assets, such as bonds, might go up. In another scenario, real estate might go down, but foreign bonds might go up.

Many studies have shown that key asset classes are not perfectly correlated with each other. Think of the major asset classes as things such as stocks, bonds, real estate investments, and cash-like investments, such as money market deposits or funds. Asset classes don't have prices that move perfectly together. There might be some positive correlations, which mean that on average if one price goes up, the other often does too, and the same on the downside. This is true of stocks in general, and even of U.S. stocks compared to foreign stocks. However, the correlation is far less than perfect.

The key to figuring out asset allocation in your portfolio is to find out what kind of a risk-taker you are. There are simple surveys you can take that try to measure if you are conservative and hate even moderate risk or if you are a risk-taker and can go for a more aggressive asset allocation. More aggressive generally means more assets that are, on average, higher risk but come with higher returns, such as stocks versus bank deposits that are extremely safe.

If you can hire a financial planner or consultant, he or she can administer a risk profile survey.

After you determine what level of risk you can tolerate, you need to spread your investments across five asset classes:

- Domestic stocks diversified across industries and size of firms (small-, mid- or large-cap; cap, which stands for capitalization, means the total value of the firm's outstanding shares on the stock market).

- Foreign stocks, both in advanced economies, such as Europe and Japan, and in emerging market nations, such as Asia, Latin America, Eastern Europe, and Africa.

- Bonds, including TIPS (Treasury Inflation-Protected Securities), because of the risk of unanticipated deflation or inflation. We discuss this more later in the chapter.

- Cash-type safe and liquid assets, such as money market funds and various kinds of bank deposits.

- Real estate, owned both directly and in Real Estate Investment Trusts (REITs).

For decades, people have been counseled to become more conservative with investments as they age, which usually means putting a larger share of wealth in fixed income investments. Those investments include whole life insurance products and bonds, as well as deposits that fit in the cash asset class. However, there are problems with becoming too reliant on bonds and fixed income investments, no matter what your age. Thus, important parts of any modern portfolio are the first two asset classes: domestic stocks and foreign stocks.

Domestic Stocks

Nearly all wealth or retirement portfolios are built around an allocation of stocks. Domestic stocks are extremely popular with many investors, perhaps due to fear of the unknown. When you build the domestic stock component of your overall portfolio, you should follow the same rule that led you to split your wealth into various asset classes: diversify.

If you buy individual stocks, it is important to diversify over a few key dimensions. Remember the technology stock crash of 2000–2002? That was a brutal reminder to diversify among a variety of sectors, including consumer goods, energy, financial services, and healthcare. Overemphasis on a sector is risky because it could fall onto hard times or out of favor.

Next, diversify with small-, mid-, and large-cap stocks. The stocks of huge firms, such as GE and Microsoft, have performed well for decades, but you need to give yourself a chance to buy into the small firms that might become big. Holding all large-cap stocks in a portfolio would mean you are missing out on the possible fast growth opportunities of small firms. Holding all small caps would be risky as these stocks are usually more volatile than large blue-chip stocks. You should own some of both.

This advice also holds if you follow the mutual fund approach to establishing stock allocations. There are mutual funds that are sector-specific. If you go for a technology fund, for example, make sure you also diversify into other sector funds or more general funds. Similarly, it makes good sense to diversify by spreading your overall domestic stock allocation over large-, mid-, and small-cap mutual finds.

▪▪▪ Foreign Stocks

International investing is popular for good reasons. Foreign stock markets do not correlate perfectly with U.S. domestic stock markets. Therefore, if the U.S. market is down a lot, there is a good chance some foreign stock markets are up (though plenty do track Wall Street closely).

You can distribute your risk by diversifying into foreign stocks. Some emerging market stocks offer high expected returns due to economic growth rates that are much faster than in the U.S. Nothing comes free in any market—the higher expected returns come with higher risks.

Investing in emerging markets brings risk of corruption, currency devaluation, and political risk. Thus, emerging markets deserve some, but not a large, part of your allocation in foreign stocks.

Usually, a larger part of your allocation in foreign stocks will go to stocks in advanced markets, such as Japan, Western Europe, Canada, and Australia. Just as you would not put all your stock allocation in one company, you should not put your money in just a few foreign companies or even markets. It is hard to know enough about particular foreign companies and markets to choose the likely winners—to target just a few is risky business. Mutual funds are likely the way to go. Mutual funds exist for individual nations, for particular regions such as Latin America, for all emerging markets, or for all foreign markets.

Overall, history has shown that steady, long-term investors with a large portion of wealth, including retirement accounts, invested in stock markets around the world have done well. If you are too conservative and hold only cash and fixed income investments, such as bonds, you miss out on growth opportunities, not to mention that your savings will more likely be eroded over time by inflation.

▪▪▪ Bonds

Fixed-income investments do have a place in the portfolios of most Americans, particularly those reaching higher ages. However, there are two big problems with these investments.

First, over recent years, interest rates have been at rather low values historically. These interest rates are not high enough to generate the kind of growth that makes compounding exciting, yielding the gains shown in the last chapter. How can anyone get excited about deposits or treasury bills yielding only 3 percent to 4 percent returns?

Many investors have tried reaching for some extra yield in the form of longer-term bonds that usually offer higher interest rates. Not a good idea. Longer-term bonds are not any safer than stocks. The longer you hold a bond, the more vulnerable you are to inflation eroding the value of your bond. This is because bonds are normally fixed in dollar terms.

Additionally, unanticipated inflation can cost you money, because higher inflation can cause higher interest rates to compensate for these inflationary pressures. Higher interest rates cause bond prices to decline, since investors will want to sell off their current bond holdings to grab new bonds issued that pay these higher rates. The result is that you might see your longer-term bonds fall in value, just like the risk in stocks. In today's uncertain markets, it is best to stick to bonds with maturities of less than five years and keep to government securities or investment-grade issues (for example, those with the best credit ratings).

Because the value of long-term bonds can be eroded by unexpected rises in inflation, shouldn't the U.S. government's Treasury Department offer a bond that protects investors from inflation? The answer is yes, and the government did just that by creating Treasury Inflation-Protected Securities, or TIPS, available since 1997.

These were originally named "Treasury Inflation-Indexed Securities" because the TIPS "index," or link, the bond's principal to the Consumer Price Index (CPI, a tool used to measure inflation). If the CPI goes up, the bond's principal value goes up proportionally. For example, if you hold a $10,000 bond at the beginning of the year and during the year inflation was 3 percent, the bond's principal adjusts up in two steps to $10,300 (rising 3 percent in value). Your income will also go up, as the dollar amount of the interest paid to you is also indexed and thus adjusted up by 3 percent.

Of course, if the CPI goes down, meaning that deflation is occurring, the principal is reduced. TIPS are adjusted every six months to match the CPI. This mechanism is called indexing, but the motivation and benefit for you is the protection against inflation.

Fortunately, you cannot lose while holding TIPS. If consumer prices go up, you get compensated for this inflation. If prices decline, otherwise known as deflation, your principal declines *but* only if you sell early. If you hold the TIPS to maturity, the Treasury guarantees you will at least get the original principal back.

TIPS can be a useful player in the portfolios of many people; especially if they are older people who saved well and do not need fast, risky growth. TIPS also entail less risk than conventional bonds due to their lower volatility.

You should analyze the fit of TIPS within your own needs. TIPS can make up a good portion of needed diversification into some fixed income in your portfolio. Also, look into inflation-indexed savings bonds, named I-bonds, which offer tax-deferred benefits and are available in small denominations, so you don't need to invest a lot at once. To learn more or to consider investing in TIPS and I-bonds, go to the www.TreasuryDirect.gov website. TIPS or I-bonds could arguably make up 10 percent or more of the portfolio of younger people, who normally should direct more of their wealth into riskier, higher return stocks. For older investors looking for more security and protection against unanticipated inflation, TIPS could be about 20 percent of their wealth allocation.

■■ ■ Cash-Type Investments

It is always a good idea to hold some of your investments in liquid accounts. This is generally your money for a rainy day. You can also put the money you *plan on investing* later into these accounts so that you earn at least a small, nominal return while you decide where to diversify your funds. You can put the cash into liquid investments, such as savings in a money market fund.

▰▪ Real Estate

Let us now consider real estate investments. There are two ways to invest in real estate, and each is useful as part of a well-diversified portfolio.

The first way to invest in real estate, naturally, is by directly owning your own home. Your home is still the best tax deal you can get on an investment. If you live in your home for at least two years and then sell, you can rake in those profits tax-free—a much better deal than if you sold a stock in two years and had to pay a 15 percent capital gains tax.

If you are like most Americans, you probably have much, or all, of your wealth in the equity of your home. Second homes, usually vacation houses at the beach or in the mountains or some other type of resort, have proven to be wonderful investments for some people. However, you must be careful about analyzing the local real estate markets. Housing prices have been gaining substantially over the past several years, and there are growing fears of a future bursting of a potential "speculative bubble" in some markets.

The U.S. population is and will keep rising, due to factors such as continued immigration and the children and grandchildren of Baby Boomers, which will support the housing market into the future. With so many Baby Boomers due to retire over the next few decades—buying up homes in key vacation areas and downsizing to smaller houses—it's unlikely you will see a nationwide housing bubble burst, but there will be some areas hard hit. The best thing to do is search out areas that are emerging rather than hitting hot spots everyone knows about already.

The second way to invest in real estate is through REITs. REITs provide diversification, both for real estate and for your overall portfolio. You can buy into commercial real estate or residential properties or invest in particular sectors of the property market that you think will do well, such as office buildings, hotels, or shopping malls, using REITs.

REITs were created in 1960. REITs allow you to invest in a company that develops, buys, manages, and sells real estate. Since the mid-1990s, REITs have gained favor as an asset class by providing reliable income. By law, to benefit from tax advantages that have helped make REITs such an attractive investment, REITs must pay out at least 90 percent of their taxable income (rents on the buildings mainly) to shareholders in the form of dividends. Older investors, in particular those looking for income when retired, have gained from the steady, relatively high level of income REITs pay out as dividends.

The returns investors earned on REITs have generally exceeded that of bonds and money market accounts, and this advantage increased in favor of REITs in the early 2000s. REITs dividends on average grew 6 percent annually in the 12 years before 2005, exceeding the average consumer price inflation of 2.5 percent, thereby offering investors consistent and increasing income while protecting capital and income streams from inflation.

Financial professionals see REITs as a useful part of most investors' portfolios because of excellent returns and the benefits of diversification. In the past, REITs have had extremely low correlations with returns on bonds or stocks. Thus, even though real estate and REIT prices in themselves contain some risk, REITs can help reduce overall risk as part of a portfolio. For example, when stocks plunged in the early 2000s, the market value of REITs actually increased, offering some wealth protection for investors who were well diversified.

Of course, the same lesson applies: You should always diversify widely and not place too much weight on any asset class. Even an asset class that has performed well in the past can suffer down years. Given that real estate has already made some nice gains in recent years, many professionals are allocating at least 10 percent, but no more than 20 percent, of client portfolios in REITs. The key in a market such as this, where most prices have increased, is to look for REITs that are not highly leveraged with debt and have an experienced and successful management team.

There are two types of REITs: publicly traded, where the price can change every day as it is listed on, for example, the New York Stock Exchange, and nontraded. Many people like the publicly traded REITs, which have advantages in being liquid. However, publicly-traded REITs can suffer from short-term volatility in price.

For those looking for solid income plus a long-term hedge against inflation, nontraded REITs could be an attractive option. Nontraded REITs are generally available from qualified financial consultants and advisors.

▩■ The Art of Rebalancing Your Wealth

Everyone loves a winner. Most people hear about a stock, mutual fund, or real estate speculation that has gone way up, and they want to jump on the bandwagon. Rush in, however, and you may be arriving at the bitter end of the party. Sadly, investors, including retirees who cannot afford it, often jump on when the wagon is about to slide back down the hill. The price they paid was, they learn after the fact, too expensive.

Similarly, people shun a loser. If a particular stock goes down, the natural reaction for many is to dump it. After real estate in a region turned sour and its price fell, many people want to unload it. Same for bonds, mutual funds, and whatever else falls out of favor. This sure sounds like human nature. Human nature also may explain why people waste money on things such as newsletters that claim, for a high price, to tell you which stocks or mutual funds have performed well in the past.

Sounds grand, but numerous studies by leading finance professionals and professors show that this backward-looking human nature can be harmful to your financial health. Your goal is to invest in tomorrow's winners, not yesterday's. If something increased greatly, it could be justified, but then the price gain has already happened and you missed it. However, if it went up more than is justified, say due to some speculative froth or short-term hyping, you could be setting yourself up for a loss by jumping on a bubble about to burst.

These are reasons why it's important to regularly rebalance your portfolio. Rebalancing your portfolio keeps you from making impulsive moves, such as panic-selling. Too few people rebalance their portfolios, but the ones who do it consistently are usually the ones who have their financial lives in order.

It's important that after you have your assets allocated with sensible portions into each of the major asset classes, you keep to those targets.

A younger person reading this book, say in their early 30s with a moderate tolerance for risk, might choose an allocation such as Portfolio A in the table.

Asset Class	Portfolio A	Portfolio B
Cash: Money Market, Bank Accounts, and so on	10%	15%
Domestic Stocks	30%	25%
Advanced Economy Foreign Stocks	15%	10%
Emerging Market Foreign Stocks	10%	5%
Traditional Bonds	10%	15%
TIPS	10%	15%
REITs	15%	15%

An older person, or anyone who abhors risk, might choose the more conservative Portfolio B with a less volatile mix of assets. They are willing to trade off some potentially higher returns to reduce risk.

What if foreign stocks have a great year and prices soar, whereas other asset classes you invested in stay flat or fall? Should you shift some of your wealth into foreign stocks? Sorry, just the opposite. You had a nice gain on the foreign stock part of your portfolio, but don't get greedy. If you buy more, and foreign stock prices fall back, you will get burned. The best thing to do is sell just enough of your foreign stock holdings so they again represent the target percentage of your portfolio. Put your capital gains into the rest of your portfolio so that each asset class is back to its target allocation. There, you rebalanced your portfolio. Do this at least annually—carve out time every year or ask your financial consultant to do it and report to you. This is important! When you start getting good at this, you ought to do this quarterly.

The more you rebalance your portfolio, the better your results, which can probably apply to all the advice in this book. So get started!

To Defer (or Not to Defer) Taxes

During your high-earning years, typically ages 35 through 65, you are usually advised to put as much of your savings into tax-deferred investments as you can. Depending on your eligibility, this includes accounts such as the 401(k) and traditional IRAs. This wisdom also applies to cousins of these instruments, such as Keogh plans and SEP-IRAs, which also allow you to avoid paying taxes on the money you put into these accounts.

The conventional wisdom regarding these investment accounts reflected the notions that first, you could immediately reduce your income tax; second, because the savings invested in these accounts are pre-taxed, you can make your income work better for you (because you earn returns on gross income versus net income); and third, by the time you are required to withdraw this money (principal and capital gains) and are taxed on it, say in your 70s, you will be earning much less money and therefore, your tax burden will also be lower.

All this is true, but you should not discount the use of Roth accounts, which essentially allow you to put *net income* away for retirement. The Roth IRA, and a wonderful new addition in 2006, the Roth 401(k), add attractive new opportunities. The Roth-type of savings and investment vehicles tax you upfront, but allow you to withdraw the money later, principal and capital gains, absolutely tax-free. Despite the benefits, people with relatively high incomes cannot make use of the Roth IRA. This is because, as with traditional IRAs, Roth IRAs are limited to people below an income threshold. (This threshold changes annually so check with the IRS at www.irs.gov to see what the limit is the year you read this.) However, the Roth 401(k) allows a broader set of people to make use of the features of a Roth plan, expanding limits and eligibility. Many employers have yet to offer this appealing program. Check where you work to see if the Roth 401(k) is available, and if it is not, encourage your employer to get on board!

The reason why these Roth accounts are worth checking out is that some people who work well into their 70s might not have less of a tax burden during their senior years. They may find that they earn almost as much as they did between ages 35 and 65, which means their tax rate may not fall.

Another factor to consider is the larger macro environment of the U.S. fiscal situation. Many economists expect that over the next several years, we will see higher taxes because of our growing federal debt. We give you the guts of the story here, which may inspire you to call your Senator's office and tell him or her you want some fiscal sanity and honesty. For more detail, two excellent recent books that deal with the gory reality of just how deeply the U.S. Federal government is getting into debt are *The Coming Generational Storm* by Laurence J. Kotlikoff and Scott Burns, and *Running on Empty* by Peter G. Peterson.

You will learn in these books, or here in summary form, that the U.S. is falling into a vicious circle. Record-sized federal budget deficits are accumulating into a massive federal gross debt. Federal fiscal budgets are basically tax revenues minus spending on government services, payments of interest on federal debt, and so forth. If the federal budget falls deeper into deficit, the government will have to borrow more money to pay for the shortfall, which leads to bigger interest payments. This then leads to bigger budget deficits as the government has to shell out more money for the interest payments, which then leads to more borrowing, and then more interest payments. You can see how this vicious circle can spiral out of control.

Our gross federal debt, which never reached even $1 trillion until 1981, is now above $8 trillion and it keeps growing. Mammoth fiscal budget deficits are forecast to last for at least the next several years, according to the nonpartisan Congressional Budget Office (CBO) calculations. (The CBO reports can be found online at www.cbo.gov.)

Bad enough as this sounds, it is just the tip of the iceberg. The real danger for a "fiscal mess" comes from the unfunded liabilities of the federal government, namely the promises to pay for

Medicare and Social Security benefits into the future. Experts have made several calculations with startlingly similar conclusions: We will not have enough tax revenues in the future to pay for these programs. The shortfall may be as much as $50 to $60 trillion. Yes, that is, trillions. The total U.S. economy, as measured by total national income or Gross Domestic Production (GDP), did not even reach $13 trillion in 2005.

The size of the unfunded liabilities may help explain why President George W. Bush made Social Security reform a top issue for debate in his second term. He began 2005 with a clear priority to convince the American people that Social Security should be at least partially privatized. The idea did not gain much traction. Still, this is an issue we should all learn more about so that we can participate in what will inevitably be a recurring public debate.

Gaining knowledge about the U.S. fiscal situation, including current trends and reform proposals dealing with government spending, taxes, Social Security, and Medicare, will also inform your own personal investment strategies. For example, you may not want to hold too many long-term government bonds, as the government may be forced to continue to flood the market with a supply of Treasury bonds to finance the gaping federal budget deficits.

Why does this journey into the U.S. economy and government finances matter to you? The truly scary, gargantuan, unprecedented federal debt forecast a few decades hence, greatly exacerbated by the unfunded Medicare and Social Security liabilities of the government, lead to one frightening conclusion: Tax rates will likely rise in the coming decades.

Tax increases, even in the face of voter opposition, are likely to be one tool in a package of solutions aimed at tackling the federal budget deficit. Another likely tool is cutting Medicare benefits for wealthy retirees.

So, instead of thinking the traditional way—specifically, that you will experience less tax burden in your older years—you may want to consider the fact that tax rates are likely to rise substantially in the future. It may make more sense to pay your taxes now than wait and pay later. The wise strategy for many may entail paying your tax now on savings and investing in a Roth IRA or a Roth 401(k) account. It may go against your nature to pay more tax now, but this strategy could save you a bundle in the future.

No one can forecast perfectly far into the future. However, a hypothetical example should help illustrate the previous point: The tax cuts enacted by President George W. Bush in his first term reduced the top marginal federal income tax rate to 35 percent. It is quite likely that by the time some successful young Baby Boomers reach their 70s, the top rate is likely to be 50 percent or more. It could even happen much sooner, depending on the future uncertainty both in terms of the economy and deficits and elections. Such marginal tax rates may sound too high to be possible, but the U.S. had even greater top rates before President Ronald Reagan's initiative to lower taxes.

Many young Baby Boomers may choose to continue working for the reasons of health and happiness portrayed in this book. Combining their earned income with their income generated by investments, they could easily face future income tax rates of 50 percent or more. Clearly, they may wish they had paid the 35 percent maximum rate now and used a Roth account.

Of course, many readers are not worried about earning a tremendous amount of income, or living off a lot of income from massive investments, when they reach their 70s. They are worried that they have not saved enough for retirement. In Chapter 10, "Don't Let Money Control You: Saving Smart for Lifelong Security and Success," we pointed out that it is best to start saving early. If you are 50 or above and did not have or follow this advice earlier, you may be thinking "great, but too late."

Actually, it is not too late. Studies show it is never too late to start saving aggressively. If taxes are constraining your ability to save now, and you are not over the earnings limit for IRAs, Congress has made it a lot easier to quickly build up a respectable nest egg in your IRA account. This applies to both Traditional and to Roth IRAs.

First, Congress has been steadily increasing the amount you can contribute annually. Second, if married, look into what are actually accommodating rules for each spouse to contribute to their own IRA. Even if only one spouse works outside the home, each can contribute the maximum to their own IRA, as long as the couple's combined income exceeds the total IRA contributions they both make. Third, and quite importantly, there is now a "catch-up" provision for individuals who are 50 and above. People who have reached this age and want to accelerate using tax-advantaged accounts gain an extra bonus starting in 2006.

Each spouse who is 50 or over can contribute an additional $1,000 to their Traditional or Roth IRA, for a total of $5,000 each. Thus, they can start "catching-up" to a solid nest egg by contributing a total of $10,000 to tax deductible IRAs, as long as the couple makes at least $10,000 and less than the upper income limits on eligibility.

It will take a lot of discipline to save enough of your income to fully fund IRAs for each spouse. Even better, to do this and also fund 401(k) plans if available, especially if your employer matches all or part of your contribution. In this case, the only sensible thing is to save and contribute to your 401(k), or you essentially walk away from free money contributed to your nest egg by your employer. The benefit could be a comfortable retirement rather than one where you regret not saving either early or enough. Trying to foster saving, the U.S. government is certainly creating new incentives from which we can all gain.

▪▪▪ Roger Staubach: "Captain Comeback"

As a quarterback for the Dallas Cowboys, Roger Staubach earned the nickname "Captain Comeback" because he led so many fourth-quarter comebacks to victory. The same nickname might be appropriate for someone who had three noteworthy careers in the military, sports, and business. In all three, he's been a huge success, winning the Heisman Trophy in 1963 while a quarterback in the Navy and then leading the Dallas Cowboys to two Super Bowl victories. Nowadays, he chairs a thriving and highly respected commercial real estate company. (For more information on Roger Staubach's life, see his Web site, www.Staubach.com.)

Interestingly enough, Roger started his real estate company while still playing for the Cowboys, knowing that his athletic career was not going to last forever. Many of us, as we contemplate having several careers in a lifetime, which is what the following chapter is about, should do the same: Begin preparing for your move years before you actually make it.

I worked in the off-season when I joined the Cowboys in 1969. My wife and I thought, obviously if I got hurt or something happened in my early career, you know I wasn't really a rookie. I was older because of my time serving in the Navy. It would be wise to have a career to fall back on. I wanted to get some business experience. I went to work for a real estate firm, The Henry S. Miller Company. I just worked in the off-season there and spent about eight off-seasons with The Miller Company and then started our company.

When you're young, sometimes you don't think that far ahead. I think I was very, very fortunate when I went to the Naval Academy. I knew I wanted to play baseball and football, but I also wanted to get a great education. I was thinking beyond just trying to live for the moment. When I got to the Cowboys, I knew someday

I was going to retire. I wanted to get some experience outside of just sports and football.

I did put a lot of hours into working in real estate during the off season and I stuck with it. I felt that, hey, I can do this. I'm still learning about real estate, but it's been a long time now and I stuck with it.

We hired some people out of the military that have come in their late 40s, early 50s, who adapted to our business because they made the commitment and their expectations are such that they know it's going to still take some time. You still have to pay a price to adapt to something new.

Athletes often go into retail businesses that can gain from their name recognition. I mean, John Elway was involved with car dealerships. Actually Troy Aikman really wants to build businesses and he's in some car dealerships, too. Your name, of course, is important, but what is your commitment? The other normal areas [for athletes to work in] are coaching and broadcasting, which are really great areas for athletes because, you know, you've learned a lot about the sport and you can communicate that sport to others, so it's a natural evolution.

I've really treasured my past as an athlete, and it's been important to me in business. People still relate to my days as an athlete, and it's good for our business, but I've committed to a different life, and early on, a lot of people, I'm sure, you know, said, "Well what does Staubach know about real estate?" After 30-something years, I think they know I've made a commitment to it.

Get Out of the Dilbert Syndrome When a Second Career Just Might Be the Answer

All the people we profiled in this book love their jobs.

Not all of them found their perfect job or career right out of college. Helen Gurley Brown didn't find her passion for magazine editing until she was 43. Jan Leschly was lucky enough to be a top professional tennis player from a young age, except sports careers are fast and short, so he was smart enough to retire and launch a new career at age 31.

To obtain financial freedom in the future, many people may need to continue working until approximately age 70, as discussed in earlier chapters. Here is the catch, though, that makes this prospect so unappealing to many folks. A good portion of us do not like our jobs. According to the latest job satisfaction survey by the Conference Board, a highly respected business group, only one in seven people are "very satisfied" in their jobs. For every age group and income range in the survey, job satisfaction levels declined since 1995. Among people aged 45 to 54—Baby Boomers—job satisfaction fell to 47.7 percent from 57.3 percent a decade earlier. It looks as if we've been on a steady descent of happiness in our jobs over the past 10 years.

If you are unhappy in your job, this chapter is for you. Take pride and money out of the equation and consider the question: Does your job truly satisfy you? Be brutally honest. Are you often jealous of other people who seem to have better, more exciting careers than you? Do you feel like you have this entrepreneurial itch that you can't ignore? Most importantly, are you bored at work? Do the hours drag by?

The reason why this matters so much is job dissatisfaction leads to unnecessary stress. Stress, as you've been told many times over, has a powerful impact on your health. That, in turn, affects your ability to age well. In a 1995 study, for instance, researchers at the University of Pittsburgh found that high levels of job stress contributed to elevated fibrinogen levels. Fibrinogen levels reflect your body's blood clotting ability and abnormally high levels are believed to contribute to coronary heart disease.

The only solution to this problem is to love what you do. It sounds so simple and yet it is one of the toughest things to figure out. Most of us are prevented from pursuing our true passion because of money. Either we are paid too much to change careers or we are paid too little to bear the cost of a transition so we can make the jump. The other reason is that many of us may not know what we truly want to do with our lives until we are well into our 40s or even 50s, a time when we believe we are too old or settled to leap into something new.

The traditional view has been to grin and bear it. It was not so long ago that most people didn't think about a career as fulfilling a passion; it was to put food on the table and to provide an education for your children. This is still the case for many people, but with burgeoning career options every year, the possibility of turning your passion into an actual vocation is becoming increasingly possible. Remember that with each passing decade, our economy is turning from a manufacturing, repetitive work type to one fueled by services, technology, and intellectual capital. This means the job choices open today did not exist 20 to 30 years ago. This is not to take away from those whose passions may very well be to farm or assemble cars, but rather that for tens of millions of people who didn't have many choices before, the situation is brighter for each generation.

The story of Doreen Linneman and her mother Carol is a perfect example. Doreen is a successful healthcare consultant who left her job at a large Fortune 500 healthcare company to start her own business, the Riverbend Group. Both women admire each other for different reasons. Doreen, who is 33 years old, looks up to her mother for quitting her nursing job and raising the kids. Carol, who is 66 years old, admires her daughter for taking the plunge to start her own business. After talking with Carol, you can tell how impressed she is with the vast opportunities open to her daughter:

I see the difference between Doreen and myself. She has much more education than I do and it really shows in the people you meet. She's a strong networker. She's in contact with people all the time. I never had that opportunity and I regret that. I think that [with more education], I probably would have been a stronger person and had more self-confidence to go out on my own in business.

Having seen Doreen's accomplishments, Carol is now entering the work force again after decades of absence. Six years ago, encouraged by her family, she went back to school and graduated with a masters of science in administration with certification in gerontology. Focused on helping people grapple with long-term care issues, Carol has used the latest self-publishing services to publish a book, which she uses at her talks discussing caregiving. Carol has also launched a Web site, www.supportgiver.com, to expand her own consultancy business. Carol proudly says:

I intend to grow my career. I have set goals for my business. My family's been wonderful in helping me. I published my book. I now have a Web site and a second guide on the way. I don't intend to slow down. My husband and I are embarking on a new adventure in living.

Now, Doreen is the one impressed by her mother's new career ambitions, one that her mother could not even imagine doing 30 years ago. Carol's life has made Doreen less apprehensive about growing older:

My mother is a phenomenal woman. A lot of women say that about their moms, but my mom is very special. Seeing now how my mom is in this life stage where the world is her oyster, who knows what I'm going to do next. I see people running marathons out there in their 80s and beyond. I'd love to be the oldest tri-athlete out there!

So how do *you* switch careers? The first step is to look inside your own situation because everybody is different. Are you interested in doing something completely opposite to your current skill set, such as going from being an accountant to a French chef? That would require a return back to school to learn new skills and very likely a big pay cut initially. Or do you want to do something less drastic, such as a move from sales to marketing within your organization?

If you fall in the latter group, the first thing to do is investigate what new opportunities might be available at your current company. More companies are open to horizontal moves if you show them you have the passion and drive to succeed in a new area. See if you can work out a plan with your current employer to eventually move into a position in which you can be happier and more fulfilled.

What if you're like many Americans and just don't know what it is you want to do? At that point, you need to get in touch with your strengths and weaknesses and see what career best suits you. Your local library and bookstores offer many books that can give you a start on assessing your personality traits and interests, which will help you pinpoint what kind of job or jobs fit you. One good book is the classic *What Color Is Your Parachute?* by Richard Nelson Bolles. Frequent new editions still sell massively, even after 30 years! It's clear, concise, and encouraging without being patronizing.

▰▰ Real People, Real Stories 1—Pete Kastner: Turning Hobby into Business

Several years ago, Peter Kastner's employer offered buyout packages as the company tried to downsize the workforce.

Peter, a hospital administrator, had always wanted to start his own business and took this as his last chance to go out on his own. Now or never, he thought. Armed with a fairly generous buyout offer, Peter "retired" from his career helping run hospitals and quickly began to launch his online antique map business. Restoring antique maps was a boyhood passion for Peter. Now working for a company of one, Peter is much happier doing what he loves to do, and he gets paid for it.

The idea of having my own business always appealed to me. I was having a particularly difficult time with managing a facility out of Framingham, Massachusetts, an old military hospital. It was a real pain in the neck and not a pleasant period for me, and I noticed on one of my visits there that there was a donut shop for sale—a Dunkin Donuts franchise. It occurred to me the guy who owned the donut shop was probably making as much money as I do. How complicated could it be in the morning to make a decision between apple or blueberry donuts? I was thinking about buying it and my wife stopped me. She said, "Oh no, you wouldn't want to do this." But the idea of me owning my own company was nice.

I retired in the spring of 2002 and I was almost 58 when I switched [careers]. I spent a week with my sister learning how to do restoration work. She's a graphic designer. One of the advantages I did have getting into the field [of restoring antique maps] was when I was an undergrad [student]. I took a couple of art courses. That was a big help.

I took a course in American architecture. The guy teaching the course was a preservationist, and he spent some time getting into restoration. Then, there were all of the things I had to learn about using the computer and that was challenging. I hired someone to come in for a couple of hours a month to go over the computers correctly, and then a friend came and started a web page for me and developed a module that I could follow.

It cost about $30,000 for the initial investment. The first year I lost money because I had to buy all this equipment. The second *year was close and now it's making a profit. It's doing okay. I can see the growth curve and I'm doing fine. The financial goal I had was to initially make up the difference between what I was earning full time and the various pensions I had, and I've pretty much done that. But I try to be disciplined. I had to make a decision between this being an actual hobby and an actual business and not get carried away by just collecting every antique map I could find.*

I really feel great about doing this. When I'm working in Photoshop, restoring the maps, if you're in the right rhythm, it's nice, it's meditative. I work three CDs worth of time in the morning. I take a little break after that. I enrolled in the Brandeis lifelong learning program and have been taking courses there in the afternoons. Sometimes, I visit clients or just take a bike ride. I'm generally happier. I get nice comments from people who either buy the work or see it, and that's really satisfying. As an administrator, people don't come in and say you have a really nice budget or they noticed the meals were delivered on time.

The business is reaching a point where I could conduct it from a laptop from anywhere in the world. If I just train someone to do the actual fulfillment, I could see myself making a transition at some point, spending some time away as long as it's near a FedEx center. We have a friend who's been running a successful gift business from Bali. That sounds nice.

There are also a variety of surveys or tests you can take to help you discover the type of work that can make you happy. You can click online and find some sources for such surveys that you can take for a small fee. For more in-depth testing, you can pay more to take tests and even receive personal counseling from various firms. Ask around for recommendations to ensure you are getting good value. These tests basically help you learn more about your personality and what sorts of jobs or industries best fit your type.

Perhaps the best known and most widely used instruments are those that have been validated and updated for decades and are available at CPP.com. CPP, Inc. provides the leading low-cost test, the Strong Interest Inventory. This assessment tool was introduced in 1927 by E.K. Strong, a researcher at Stanford University. It has the double advantage of being validated over a long period of time with large samples of people, while being frequently updated and revised to reflect new testing techniques as well as changing or new occupations. The same firm provides the Myers-Briggs Type Indicators, which many readers may have either taken or know about. The test will let you know about key features of your personality and how this style matches up with your career choice. The leading example reveals if you are an extrovert or an introvert. Obviously, an introvert should not be in most types of sales but may make a good accountant.

▰▰ Real People, Real Stories 2—Carol Gee Pursues Her Dream of Writing Books

Carol Gee has had several careers but only one has captured her heart: being an author.

Born in the South, Carol grew up with little means and very limited career choices. She clearly loved writing at an early age, but had to settle for different career paths to support herself and her family.

With no money for college, Carol took a job after high school at a Virginia shoe factory. After several years, she decided the Air Force would offer a way out of the dead-end job. She joined the military, and after years of service, she used the GI Bill to obtain a college education. She earned a master's degree in management and human relations from Webster University in St. Louis, Missouri.

Though earning a nice income as an editor and manager at Emory University, Carol never forgot her dream of being a published author. This was her passion. She continued to write and write, sending manuscript after manuscript out despite receiving mounds of rejection letters. Finally, InnerLight Publishing in Atlanta accepted her manuscript for *The Venus Chronicles*, a humorous guidebook for women, fulfilling her decades-long dream of becoming a published book author. *The Venus Chronicles* (venuschronicles.net), quickly sold out its first printing, and Carol is now working on an audio book version.

Carol was lucky to know early what her true passion was and, despite the odds, was able to follow her dreams by remaining resilient. Switching careers is never easy, but with persistence, it can happen.

Because Carol is a gifted writer, she gives us her thoughts on following your passion in her own words:

My love affair with books began at an early age, and I read everything that I could get my hands on. Books introduced me to new friends, new things, and they carried me away to places that I never knew existed. As I read, I also daydreamed of some day writing books that people would love.

Growing up, I wrote little stories to teach my younger sister to read. Clearly a savant, she could add large sums in her head but had problems reading See Dick Run *and* Green Eggs and Ham. *As I got older, I wrote poems to vent my frustrations as a single woman. A few of them won honorable mention in contests (but no money).*

I joined the Air Force at age 20 and stayed for more than 20 years. During that time, I recorded my military experiences, filling page after page in a loose-leaf notebook. Other jobs followed after I left the Air Force, including spending a brief stint as a mental health counselor.

While my life veered off into several directions, I never lost sight of my dream. Still it took a big, big, big birthday staring me in the face (along with that one gray chin hair that persisted in growing back even after yanking it out with industrial-strength tweezers) to catapult me into finally following my dream.

Ideas for my books and columns pop into my head at the oddest moments, (when I am brushing my teeth and even in my sleep), while the ambrosial strains of humor and irreverence float throughout my thoughts like incense. I jot notes down on anything that is handy, from Post-it Notes to paper napkins. I use whatever writing instrument I can find at the moment: a pencil, a Magic Marker, or a Sharpie. Once not having any of them ready, I used the lip liner pencil that I discovered residing in the bottom of my purse. That it had some gunky stuff stuck to it (gum, I hope) and that my words peeked out from a wine shade mattered not one wit.

I admit jotting stuff on Post-its is a mite risky. Still, I love living dangerously. For example, one morning my husband awoke to discover a Post-it stuck smack dab in the middle of his forehead, as I have been known to jot down an errant thought in the middle of the night lest I can't get back to sleep. It's true: Post-its do stick to anything.

Writing is not for the faint of heart. You have to really love it. Over the years, I have had enough rejection slips to wallpaper my guest bathroom. There have been tough times that shook my confidence to the core, times where I felt like publishers had ripped open my soul and tap danced on it. Those were the times that I admonished myself to stick to whatever day job I had. But writing was in my blood. And when the heart harbors a secret passion, nothing else matters.

Before I knew it, I would find myself jotting down notes for an article or penning a little short story to entertain my kindergartners as a substitute teacher in places like South Carolina or even as far away as the lush jungles of Panama. Two fairy tales, The Magic Cookies *and* Snowflake Soup, *still lie dormant in my desk drawer in my home office. I have vowed recently to dust them off, submit them somewhere, and see what happens.*

In homage to my former career as a counselor, I liken my writing as "therapy, but without the couch." Stories I once wrote in my head now practically write themselves down on paper. By exploring a multitude of experiences and dabbling in varied occupations and interests, I continue to find my inspiration from everyday living.

Throughout the many twists and turns in my life, I've finally done it. I have become a writer. F. Scott Fitzgerald once said, "There are no second acts in American lives." Baby Boomers my age and older are dispelling that notion daily by reinventing themselves, proving that American lives do have second acts. If Lady Luck smiles on you like she has done on me, you get to inspire people. If you are really, really lucky, you even make them laugh.

There are quite a few reputable firms that provide deeper assessments or more comprehensive consulting services for those searching for a better fit in a second career. For example, numerous experts cited Right.com/global/consult/assess/ or Birkman.com as firms with proven results over many years. You will need to assess for yourself what depth of personal testing and career consulting you can afford. Of course, some of you will have access to free consulting as part of packages if you leave a firm that has downsized.

Ed Case, a Boston attorney for 22 years, took an aptitude test several years ago at Johnson O'Connor Research Foundation (jocrf.org), which cost approximately $600, when he was considering switching careers. "When I was in my 40s, I was thinking about what else I could do," he says. "I found out my strongest aptitude was to be a nonfiction writer—taking facts and reorganizing them, which was ironic because that's also suitable for a litigator." After more soul searching, Ed decided to quit his job and plunge into the hectic world of nonprofits. He now runs an organization called Interfaith Family and is much happier directing a nonprofit than making closing arguments in court.

Money may be relatively tight, but getting a good personal assessment and evaluation of what makes you unique can be the most crucial and best investment you make. An idea you might not have thought of and one that turns a sour lemon situation into lemonade is if your firm is trying to downsize, you can offer to help reduce head count if they would be willing to give you a good exit package that includes some training for a new career.

Along with formal assessments, take time to talk to friends who know you best and try to find opportunities to observe professionals who work in fields that might ignite the inner passion in you. Consider that you might have to go back to school or take a lower paying job to get into the right career. Ultimately, you must trust what both your heart and head tell you so that you can find your true vocation.

If you don't want to take any tests or can't afford them, you can still get plenty of ideas about new career paths just by turning to, surprisingly, government websites. This is one way you can make your tax dollars work for you.

A crucial website for people who look for a more fulfilling career is the U.S. Department of Labor's Bureau of Labor Statistics (bls.gov). You may want to turn to bls.gov/emp/, which has many links to lists of hot growth industries and jobs. There are even descriptions of the education and training you'll need for these hot careers. Check out bls.gov/emp/emptab3.htm and also emptab4.htm, which list the most likely occupations to grow over the next decade. Another website, careeronestop.org, has a lot of useful information and is a partnership between federal and state governments.

Jobs Posted: Only 65 and Older Need Apply

We realize that for some of you who are in your 60s and maybe even your 70s, it's not simple to switch careers—much less find a new job after you have retired.

If you think all is lost, hang on. The fact that America's elderly population is growing tremendously each year means that companies are finally waking up to the reality of a viable "older" work force.

It also means there's a vast amount of resources available to help older Americans explore job opportunities that were not present even 10 to 15 years ago.

One of the biggest resources is AARP, which was formerly known as the "American Association of Retired Persons." The group now goes by its acronym because it felt the full name was too geriatric-sounding and didn't reflect the active personalities of its millions of members.

AARP's website, aarp.org, has now been designed to help people over 50. Its core membership focuses on taking control of their aging in many ways, including finding new and rewarding careers. One example is implementing a program with leading online career site Monster.com to help people over 50 find suitable jobs. Both partners are developing a variety of channels to help connect mature job seekers with jobs in their own local regions.

Some big companies "get it" in terms of hiring older workers. Every study documents the value to the company when workers have a great deal of prior experience. Only about 10 percent of jobs in our modern, service-based economy require physical strength. For the rest of the jobs, wisdom, which can usually be won only through long experience, trumps physical strength needs.

The AARP has a section on its website that highlights the Featured Employers Program, which recognizes companies that hire older workers. The good news is these companies are major employers, most being national in scope. Most offer the flexible schedules that the older worker often desires, so they can work part-time or travel for extended periods as well as work on other projects. Many also offer full health insurance. The leading companies are household names, such as The Home Depot, Borders Group, MetLife, Pitney Bowes, Walgreens, and AlliedBarton.

The Home Depot has received awards and favorable press for a number of innovative programs, such as one that allows seniors to work near their home in the North in summer, switching to a Home Depot in the South if they live in the South (such as Florida) in the winter. Home Depot's executive vice president of human resources, Dennis Donovan, along with Chairman and CEO Bob Nardelli, are credited with introducing a series of creative hiring partnerships with nonprofit and government agencies (other examples include programs for military persons and their spouses).

Donovan suggested that older associates tend to have a better attendance rate and a longer tenure with the company. Donovan states, "There are so many intangibles our mature associates bring to the workplace. Generally speaking, they bring a tremendous wealth of knowledge from previous jobs, and the majority of them bring a sense of leadership, an incredible benefit. They have an admirable flexibility when it comes to scheduling, and many are working in our stores because they just enjoy the experience and want to be a part of our team."

If the previous companies or jobs don't appeal to you, there are still other resources to tap just by clicking online. Here are three of our favorites:

- Experience Corps (www.experiencecorps.org)—Tutoring and other opportunities in public schools and after-school programs in 14 cities. "Volunteers" age 55 and up are often paid small stipends to work 15 or more hours a week. (We mentioned the program in Chapter 8, "Socialize Your Way to Health.")

- Retired Brains (www.retiredbrains.com)—This site includes part-time, full-time, and temporary job listings for retirees.

- Senior Job Bank (www.seniorjobbank.org)—This site includes job listings for those over 50.

More detailed career information is provided at bls.gov/ooh in the *Occupational Outlook Handbook*, which provides valuable assistance to individuals making decisions about their future work lives. Revised every two years, the *Handbook* describes what workers usually do on the job, general working conditions, the training and education required, earnings, and the expected job prospects in a wide range of industries.

After you figure out what you want to do, focus on making it happen. You know the saying that when one door closes, often another one opens? Well in the same vein, after that door opens, close it behind you and throw away the key. Don't pursue this new career with the idea that you can always leave again. You will never succeed this way.

Likely your first step after you determine what you want to do is to go back to school for some training. Zig Ziglar talked to us about the virtues of "learning on the go," and that it is the lifelong learners who will always remain employed. He is absolutely right. Education does not stop at 21. It is something you must continue doing for the rest of your life. (It is also the way to keep your mind sharp.)

▪▪▪ Real People, Real Stories 3— Hilde Gerst: Art Gallery Owner, Filmmaker, Inspiration

Hilde Gerst is a most refreshing lady to meet. She is living a very full life, beginning before World War I in Silesia, a region of Austria that was transferred to Poland after the war. Witness to many of the major events for a good part of the past century, Hilde Gerst has been a documentary filmmaker, facilitator of intellectual and cultural dialogue, wife, mother, and world-renowned art dealer.

Hilde Gerst was married to a Viennese doctor and had two children when in 1939 she correctly foresaw the coming Second World War and Holocaust. Months before the invasion of Poland, she led her family to safety in New York.

With a voracious appetite to learn about new cultures, Hilde eventually became a documentary filmmaker, traveling literally around the world every nine months and producing highly regarded films. In particular, by gaining access through the U.S.

State Department, she befriended the heads of state of nearly every nation in Southeast Asia.

It was during these travels that Hilde learned more about art and antiques. Eventually, she started collecting the work of artists she had the talent to identify as up-and-comers, and before she knew it, she became an art dealer. Starting from scratch, Hilde has built a gallery known the world over for displaying such exquisite art from the likes of Picasso and Renoir in the Hilde Gerst Gallery on 987 Madison Avenue in New York.

Though her life now is very glamorous and extraordinary, Hilde started from nothing and is an inspiration to all of us who are fearful of pursuing multiple careers. She is proof that having several careers can lead to an exciting and successful life.

I'm in my art gallery six days a week for six hours each day. I don't open until 11 a.m. because I say, "The people who can afford my paintings don't need to get up early."

I built my business myself, against all advice. Everyone said, "You are not a business woman, you will lose your shirt." A year later, they all came back pleading, "Hilde, would you like to have a partner?"

The business started informally as I would bring back from Paris some pieces I liked from young artists. Back in New York, I would show the pieces at the Sunday teas I host for friends, and they would always want to buy the art.

Eventually, I started going to Paris four or five times a year to buy paintings from up-and-coming artists. On one trip, I bought 18 paintings and then prepared to rush to the airport for my return to New York. I had just enough money left for the taxi fare. But on the way out of the Bristol Hotel, a blue painting caught my eye in an expensive gallery across the street. It was so exquisite, I had to delay and go in. The painting was $10,000 back then, which my friends tell me would be the equivalent of hundreds of thousands now. It was so much more money than any painting I *had ever bought as it was by Vlaminck, and I had not dealt with the established masters before (masters meaning the truly masterful and famous artists of history).*

I returned to New York, and the next morning I was at Chase Manhattan for a loan when the bank opened. I had no securities to offer to back up the credit, but I got the loan for $10,000 based on my reputation. I wired the money to Paris, got a fabulous frame for the painting, and attempted to sell it.

My children were nervous. They said, "You now have massive debt for the first time, and you don't have the clientele for such an expensive work. Mother, you will lose your shirt."

I put the painting in an auction at the leading auction house. Well, the day of the auction, there was torrential hail. There was no one in the streets. All day, I had a terrific headache, thinking of the debt and the loss I would most likely take, and my family continuing to say that they told me so.

When the bidding time came, there were only two people in this huge room that was usually standing room only. I feared that in all likelihood they were only employees of the auction house. However, the auction started and the price quickly rose until my painting was sold for $16,500. My daughter called to ask, "How much did you lose?" I enjoyed telling her I made a profit.

It took me a few weeks to find out who the buyer was, as they would not answer my questioning at first. Eventually, someone leaked that the person with the winning bid was the First Lady, who had seen it in a private viewing at the auction house and loved it. It was Jackie Kennedy who taught me the valuable lesson I have since followed: The only way to make money is with the art works of the masters.

My greatest pleasure is to come home after working in my gallery all day. I turn on all my lights and look at every painting in my home. I can say that nobody gave me a penny. I created it all by myself.

You don't necessarily have to go back to a full-blown course schedule unless you are considering becoming a doctor or lawyer or some other profession where you need to get a degree. Most of the time, training means taking classes at the thousands of community colleges, technical colleges, vocational institutes, and universities that now cater to "adult education." What counts is not so much the name of the institution you attend, but the amount of experience and education you procure (though you, of course, want to make sure it is a reputable educational institution).

Each state sees the continuing education of its residents as crucial to the state's economic development and to the well being of its people, so resources abound. Contact your own state's department of education and also see if you have a department of technical and adult education or something with a similar name. Also, many states devote significant resources to work force development, which you can try to learn about from state agencies or even the local Chamber of Commerce. From there you will likely find a bevy of programs to tap.

Give Something Back to the Schools—Yourself!

Schools are not just a place for you to learn new skills, but also to represent a unique job opportunity.

Thousands of community and technical colleges are always looking for qualified specialists who can teach courses part time. You do not need to have a Ph.D. to teach at most of these institutions; instead, these schools look for experienced communicators who can translate their real-world knowledge to the classrooms.

Most of these schools can't afford to pay you much, perhaps a few thousand dollars for a semester. But that's not the point. If you can afford to do it, give something back by helping others launch their own careers. You'll be surprised after you start teaching how much you know of your own craft and how energetic you'll feel helping others learn.

Don't forget to tap into professional groups tied into your new career aspirations. Oftentimes, these associations offer their own classes and seminars to help members freshen up their skills. Some even offer e-learning classes, so you don't have to be physically near these groups to reap their benefits. The bottom line is with the vast array of resources out there—both online and offline—there's really no excuse in not getting all the training and education you need to make that crucial career change.

Ultimately, even minimal searching on the World Wide Web can introduce you to many free resources to help you learn about new career opportunities. The main point is that your happiness is your responsibility, so do the research to find out what you will likely enjoy doing, what you can be good at, and what the world needs. If you can find the intersection of those three things, you can likely live a long, healthy, active, happy, productive, and perhaps most importantly, meaningful life.

▥ ■ Pete Dawkins: Success From Multiple Careers

General Pete Dawkins, the great Heisman trophy-winning running back from the Army and now a senior executive at Citigroup, has succeeded in many careers. (Go to PeteDawkins.com to learn more about Pete's numerous football awards, academic success as a Rhodes Scholar and Ph.D., and family history.)

Like Roger Staubach, Pete knew that his military career would end before he was ready to retire. At 45, Pete decided to leave the military earlier than expected and try his hand at business. This turned out to be one of the best decisions he'd ever make as he quickly made a name for himself on Wall Street, working for Lehman Brothers, Bain & Company, and since 1991, Citigroup. Pete is now vice chairman of Citigroup's Private Bank, traveling globally to help lead the bank.

By relative standards, Pete is still young; he'll be 68 this year. Switching careers is nothing new in his family. His father, Henry, a dentist, retired at the ripe old age of 76. But instead of settling down, his father retired on a Saturday and was at a sculpting class that Monday! Even more amazing, Pete's father went on to start a lucrative career in sculpting at an age when most of us think we're heading to the nursing home. He lived until he was 100 years old.

I spent 24 years in the military—four years at West Point would add to that, so that would be 28 years in total—but I never thought of the military as a career. I don't think I ever thought after 6 years or 11 years or 17 years, "Well, now this is my career." That may seem jarring to you.

My career had some fast advances and then flat spots, as everybody's does. And there were pivotal points where if things had happened just a little bit differently one way or the other, I would not have had a career. But those are factual things. In terms of attitude, in terms of outlook, in terms of how I viewed my life, I have to say I loved my time in uniform.

Yet when I made the decision to leave, which was a very complicated decision, things were going very well in my life in my military career then. I had been selected to succeed Colin Powell and was about to be promoted, but I had made up my mind that as much as I looked forward to that, I really wanted to do something in addition in my life.

Because one of the things that had weighed on my mind was that in the four or five years before I decided to leave the military, I had become suddenly rather knowledgeable about a number of senior officers who were retiring or had retired—four stars, Chairman of the Joint Chiefs, what not—and I had been thinking about it for a while because something was curious. What I realized was it didn't seem to me they were very happy after they retired.

As I reflected on it, I thought that the reason they [other retirees] weren't happy was because they felt they were at the height of their power, the height of their competency—they finally developed an ability to really perform in these different functions and roles as senior general officers—and then they were retired right at the apex of their ability, just when they felt they could go on for another five or ten years.

If you were 60 years old and all you had done was be a soldier all your life, the ability at that point to go and have another life, another career was very limited. They became consultants or they would work in think tanks or something, but essentially their productive lives ended.

One of the things that was frustrating to me was I didn't want to be one of these people who at 56 years old felt as if my life was over. That was a significant part in my finally tearing myself away from a life I had come to love. My decision may seem illogical to people, but it didn't seem illogical to me.

I didn't think in terms of [switching] careers. I just thought about my life in making that initial transition. I was very conscious of the fact that life was not limitless. There were a finite number of years when you could be active and productive.

I knew I had to start that new field early enough to have enough runway ahead of me—to have 20-odd years or 25 years or 30 years—to do this new thing because achievement is a function of effort over time. It's not instantaneous and it's not spontaneous. It's effort over time.

I wasn't preoccupied with whether I had the skill base, interestingly. I think I had the confidence—even false confidence—that I could learn what I needed to do in another field. I probably wasn't going to become a brain surgeon or something that would take a long apprenticeship and training. But I just felt I could fill out my abilities and skills and intuitions by focused effort, but that I needed time to do it.

My father lived to 100. There were a couple of secrets that I learned, or lessons I observed from my father. One was he always had a project. He was a dentist and one of the merits was that dentists had regular hours. It's not like being on call. So, when he came home from work, he did a certain amount of reading of journals, but he wasn't an academic dentist. He kept track of things, but it didn't take the fullness of his energy. He loved to make things and build things and work with wood. He was very accomplished. Wherever we lived, there was always some home improvement project, which, again, may not seem all that striking to readers today, but 50 years ago it was unusual. It was nowhere near as common and it wasn't as easy to get things. There were no Home Depots in those days.

I've always sort of adopted that strategy and normally have half a dozen projects that I'm working on sometimes. Right now, I'm too busy to, say, build a cupboard, but I'd think about it and design and work on it and oversee it.

Second was he had real focus; he became absorbed by things. When he became involved in something, he became completely involved in it. He didn't dabble in it. He didn't just do it a little bit. It absorbed him. Baptism by total immersion. A great example is his sculpting.

To his dying day at 100, he never displayed any aspect of dementia. He became more limited physically and then, at the very end, quite enfeebled physically. But this only happened very late in his life. Even in the face of that, his mind was still clear and functioning.

He said something to me that struck me as being both quaint and lovely, but also very insightful. He was in his late 90s. I would talk to him almost every day, and go visit him when I could. One time I had been to visit him, and we'd had a nice chat and then there was a quiet period. He then looked at me with this sort of knowing expression, and said, "Have you noticed how really old, old people have become?" I thought about it for a minute and I thought he was fooling. I thought it was a joke. Then I realized it wasn't a joke at all. I further recognized that "old" is a relative term, not an absolute term. I believe that notion of relativeness—of age being relative not absolute—is part of the secret of understanding all of this.

Conclusion

In this book, we have shown, using the latest research and offering various role models, that it is possible to live a very long, productive, healthy, and happy life. The key is to balance everything in your life. Your money affects your health as much as your health affects your ability to earn money. A good night's sleep is as important in keeping stress at bay as having a job that you love. Everything is linked.

Some of the advice in this book is visible and tangible, which makes it easy to remember and always follow. Eat your naked foods. Fit in exercise like it's another meeting. If you can, exercise more than you need by eschewing modern conveniences. Dr. C. Everett Koop emphasized forgoing elevators and taking the stairs in your office building whenever you can. Similarly, people often waste 5 to 10 minutes a day circling parking lots looking for the space closest to the supermarket. Park a little farther away (make sure it's safe!) and walk a little.

Studies clearly show that one way to keep the brain and memory in top shape is to be physically healthy. Don't smoke, exercise, and eat a healthy diet. It's really that simple. Remember the brain really is the "use it or lose it" organ, so make sure you become a lifelong learner. Plan on working past 65, but in a job you love.

Beyond physical health and vocational challenges, it is important to remain curious and learn by reading and conversing. Charlie "Tremendous" Jones is a close friend of Truett Cathy, the inspiring business leader and philanthropist. Charlie received his nickname because of his tremendous energy, enthusiasm, care for others, charity, and spiritual nature. He has given many thousands of speeches all over the world, as he is still in great demand at age 77 as a motivational speaker. He is best known for this line: "You are the same today as you will be in five years, except for two things: the people you meet and the books you read."

Think about this, live by it, change for the better by it. Charlie points out that all the great men and women he has known were readers with a purpose. They never read for enjoyment. They read for a purpose, either to learn to be more effective in their work or to learn to share with people.

Truett Cathy's Tips For Life

After Colonel Sanders, Truett Cathy is probably the other guy best known for his chicken. The chicken sandwich, that is.

Founder of Chick-fil-A®, Truett is credited with "inventing" the chicken sandwich that millions line up for at his restaurants. Garnished with just a pickle, the simple sandwich has its devotees all over the country, some of whom have been known to travel hundreds of miles to buy his sandwiches.

Truett has always been something of an oddity in the business world and especially in the fast-paced, cut-throat arena of the fast-food industry. Openly religious, Truett keeps his restaurants closed on Sundays despite losing crucial revenues. He's also a long-time champion of higher education, with Chick-fil-A having been the first fast-food services company in 1973 to offer its employees college scholarships. To date, the company has awarded over $20 million in scholarships. He and his wife also have 135 foster children through their Winshape Foundation, which pays couples to stay home and provide love and care to foster children.

At 84, Truett maintains the same type of folksy sense of humor and down-to-earth persona that characterizes his company. Being a self-made success, Truett often gets asked how he's made his millions while still holding true to his values.

Here's his take on how to make life work:

- Excitement keeps life going. There's a difference between a workaholic and a person excited about what they're doing. People like to follow people who are excited, not people who are workaholics.
- If you fall in love with your work, you don't have to work any longer.
- Your relationship [with your wife or husband] is a very vital part of success. It will make you or break you. A business person needs that support. My wife has put up with a lot. A lot of times she didn't know when I would come home. She became a master of operating the microwave. Just like tonight. I just called her to tell her I wouldn't be home so we could finish this interview, right?
- There's no problem that doesn't have a solution to it.
- Failure is often just another step you take to reach success. Most people I've known that have amounted to anything have been through times of doubt and nonproductivity, but yet they have a desire to achieve something noteworthy.
- To stay healthy and live a long life, the number one rule is "eat more chicken."

To help you read with a purpose, we asked the people we interviewed what they would recommend you read. Some cited the Bible of course. Others mentioned *Gandhi, An Autobiography: The Story of My Experiments With Truth*. One common genre was biographies; many people we interviewed were reading or just finishing reading biographies of historical leaders, such as John Adams, Benjamin Franklin, and Alexander Hamilton.

Business leaders also turned to life stories for inspiration, such as *Long Walk to Freedom: The Autobiography of Nelson Mandela*. Tom Johnson joined Donald Keough and others in praising the autobiography of the late Katherine Graham, *Personal History*. Tom stated, "It was the most open, honest, comprehensive autobiography I've ever read."

Roger Staubach and others with military experience mentioned a number of good books on wars and those who fight them. One book many mentioned deals with the strategy at Gettysburg, *The Killer Angels*. Tom Johnson, also a veteran in addition to being a journalist, recommends *Charlie Wilson's War* by George Crile, and *They Marched into Sunlight* by David Maraniss. Tom said, "It brought back the most vivid memories for me of Vietnam. An incredible book."

As you've read, researchers have found that relationships are key to health and longevity. For the many people who are single, either because it is a choice or because they have not found the right partner, or they lost their spouse, friendships are crucial. Recent research shows that it is important to have a good number of friends, not just one or two close friends. The same can be said for maintaining relationships with as many members of your extended family as you can.

Research shows that married people on average tend to live longer. Many of the "aging smart" people we profiled are in a long marriage, which supports the data reported by medical research. The benefits are much greater for men and sure enough, the men we interviewed in this book all had long marriages. Dr. Koop celebrated his 67th wedding anniversary in September 2005. Others who will be married 60 years or more by 2006 include J.B. Fuqua, Zig Ziglar, and President Jimmy Carter. Don Keough and Truett Cathy have been in marriages at least 55 years. The glamorous couple, Helen Gurley Brown and David Brown, had been together over 45 years when we interviewed them.

No doubt, our sample is too small for any statistical significance, but the argument is strong for being with one person who supports and loves you. This is extremely important to your health and sanity!

Our role models are already succeeding into their late years, but will you? Luck, in the form of your genes, has a hand in your future, but a bigger role will be played by your own decisions and your own actions. Will you make the effort to eat well and to exercise your brain as well as your body? Will you make the effort to find a vocation that can fulfill you?

By following the strategies in this book, you can do a lot to increase your odds of living long and living well. To see if you are doing the right things, try out the Web site at http://www.agingresearch.org/calculator. Find the link to the "Living to 100" quiz. Try it to see a projection of your life expectancy right now. Then, see how your life expectancy changes with the modification of just a few behaviors. Surprising, right? You have so much control over your aging; it's a shame if you don't take advantage of it.

You can live a long, healthy, and prosperous life. It is up to you to do so, and we hope this book helps guide and inspire your journey. Eat smart, be smart, and most importantly, remember to just say no to pink pants!

The Baby Boomer Factor and Life Expectancy

As discussed, the impetus for this book is the aging of the Baby Boomer generation. This famous generation comprises the 76 million Americans born between 1946 and 1964, an unprecedented amount of people conceived between World War II and the Vietnam War. Given that the youngest Baby Boomers were born in 1964, by 2030 all Baby Boomers will be older than 65. The U.S. Census Bureau forecasts that there will be nearly 72 million people in the U.S. age 65 or older in 2030, almost double the number of people 65 and older now in the population. Want to get rich? Just start thinking now of the goods and services those plentiful older Americans will buy and how you can start a company that caters to their needs! By 2030, those 72 million people over 65 will amount to 20 percent of the total U.S. population (see the following figure).

This forecast is the reason why you've heard so much about reforming the Social Security and Medicare systems. It's also going to affect every aspect of U.S. life, from determining where Americans live, to the price of beach-front property, to the demand for gerontologists, to the importance of retaining people aged 65 and over in the work force.

We're not alone in experiencing the "graying" of our population. By 2030 in Japan, people over 65 will make up nearly 30 percent of the population, as the following figure illustrates. In Europe, almost a quarter of the population will be seniors by 2030. Some major countries, such as Italy, are predicted to exceed the European average and age much more than in the U.S., resembling Japan. Some Japanese and European companies are already reacting to this prospect by providing older workers with incentives to continue working past typical retirement ages. Some governments are also looking into the solvency of their pension schemes—and cutting back.

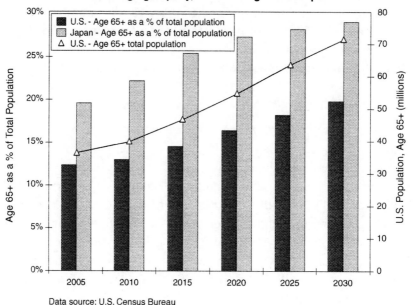

U.S. Is Aging Rapidly, but Is Younger than Japan

Data source: U.S. Census Bureau

So what's the sensible solution? For one, society must reform to make it more desirable for people to work well beyond 65, or just five more years to 70. This may entail raising the retirement age for full Social Security benefits—currently slated to increase gradually from 65 to 67—to an even later age, eventually approaching or even reaching 70. A sensible and fair solution to a looming crisis may also be to provide incentives for people to keep working beyond 65, perhaps by providing tax breaks or other financial benefits. Efforts to improve the respect and value placed on the experience and wisdom of older workers can benefit the economy and society.

If age 70 gradually becomes a benchmark for retirement, the financial future of the U.S. brightens dramatically. Age 65 made financial sense when it was largely introduced in the U.S. in 1935 with the passage of the Social Security Act, following Chancellor Otto von Bismarck's pioneering 19th century program to install government pensions in Germany.

Back then, people were far less likely to reach age 65, and the concept of retirement was still relatively new. After all, in 1935 the life expectancy at birth was only 58 for men and 62 for women. But since then, U.S. life expectancies have risen dramatically to approximately 75 years for men and 80 years for women. A pension promise in 1935 if you lived past age 65—when the average life was only 60 years—rang rather hollow. Now, a vast majority (five out of six) of Americans live to 65 or beyond. Impressively, seven out of every eight women reach the age 65 benchmark.

Note that life expectancies are measured from birth. If you have already reached age 65, you have shown evidence of good genes and smart behavior. Given this, you are expected to live even longer. Conditional upon already being 65, U.S. women are expected to live an added 19.8 years, to age 84.8. U.S. men still face a gender gap, but a smaller one at age 65 than at earlier ages because men making it to age 65 did not die young from some risky behavior. Men who are already 65 are expected on average to live another 16.8 years to age 81.8. The next figure shows conditional life expectancies for various ages for males and females in the U.S.

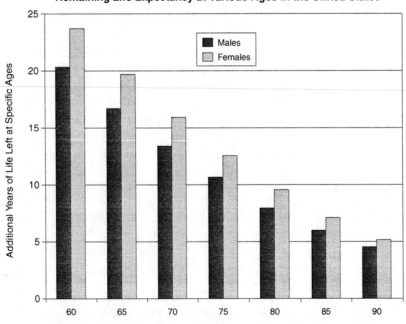

Remaining Life Expectancy at Various Ages in the United States

Data source: U.S. Centers for Disease Control, 2003 data

There are significant differences in life expectancies among key groups in the U.S., but a hopeful trend is that the gap between these groups is shrinking. Fortunately, they're shrinking because all groups are increasing their life expectancies, and the groups with the highest mortality rates are seeing rapid improvement. All the good information available about the need to stop smoking, to eat a moderate and nutritious diet, and to exercise daily is spreading more widely among the populace. We hope this book motivates people of all races—men and women—to get off the couch or push back from the dessert table.

Let's look at the two most significant gaps. Regarding gender, you can see that women live longer than men on average. Diet and excessive drinking, aggressive driving, other risky behaviors, and violence likely play roles. The good news is that men over the past couple of decades have reduced their smoking, their consumption of fatty meats, and in general, many are more heart healthy or practicing healthy habits. More good news is that the gender gap is down by one third since its 1979 peak: it is 5.3 years now, whereas women then lived fully 7.8 years more than U.S. men on average.

Second, the U.S. faces a crucial life expectancy gap that is too often ignored. There is a racial gap that has been so long-standing and serious that life expectancy statistics usually are broken down to account for the vast differences among the white and black populations. In addition, there is a great diversity in the Hispanic population, and some Hispanic people report as black, whereas others report as white. Thus, the data and terms used are as they are reported.

Life expectancy for whites in 2003 was 78, compared to 72.8 for blacks. This overall racial gap of 5.2 years is even more distressing if you look at the numbers for males only, where the white minus black gap is 6.2 years. The big issue is the relative short life expectancy of black males who trail black females by nearly 7 years and white females by over 11 years! Numerous causes have been hypothesized, including various consequences of poverty, lack of access to healthcare and adequate nutrition, risky behaviors, crime, smoking, and the much higher infant mortality rate of blacks, particularly black males.

Fortunately, the trends are favorable. The racial gap, which was 7.6 years in 1970, has diminished by almost a third since its peak in recent decades. Faster progress is no doubt desirable, but at least black life expectancy growth is outstripping the continued welcome gains for whites. Blacks still suffer disproportionately from poverty and poor access to healthcare, but there are grounds for optimism. A bright spot is the shrinking gender gap between black men and women; it was a whopping 8.9 years in 1979, but black male life expectancy has improved 5.2 years since.

Despite favorable trends, black male life expectancy is still just under 70 years. Does this mean that a general rise in retirement age toward 70 will rob black men of their retirements? No, first because life expectancy for this group should continue to rise. Second, recall that life expectancies are much higher for people who reach 70 than life expectancies calculated from birth. Tragically, many black babies die, often due to their mother's lack of access to prenatal care and proper nutrition while pregnant. The infant mortality rate for black babies before reaching age one exceeds 14 per thousand, double the overall U.S. rate. In addition, black males die at much higher rates than black females, or male or female whites, of the 18 to 35 age range. For black men who survive the hazards of these younger years, life prospects are good, although admittedly still less than for other groups.

Even with today's expectancies, plus the higher ones likely in the future, most black males who retire at 70 will have many years of retirement. Currently, black males who reach 70 will average an additional 12.2 years.

▄▄■ Working Beyond 65 and Keeping Long Retirements

Given that people in the U.S. who are 65 can generally look forward to many more years of life, it is not unreasonable to expect that most may want to keep working for a few more years. This is particularly true if society can move toward new careers for seniors that offer jobs that are both fulfilling and flexible. Otherwise, a 65-year-old woman could face a retirement of 20 or more years, which sounds great at first but may end up long, lonely, and boring. If society can make it in older people's best interests to keep working, this will lead to a positive solution to what many see as a negative or a looming crisis—the "retirement" of the Baby Boomer generation.

The following figure shows how moving to a benchmark retirement age of 70 by 2030 could boost the economy, helping the U.S. stay solvent and supplied with experienced workers; the figure uses bars to portray key ratios. The point is to highlight what could happen to the ability of the working-age population to support those who are considered more senior and thus likely to be retired. This is a key topic to the future solvency of Social Security and policy options.

The first bar shows the ratio of those of "working age," which is defined as ages 20 to 64 inclusive, to those "seniors defined as age 65 and above," in 2005. You can see why Social Security is able to run a financial surplus now because the vast majority of adults work and pay into the system. However, the second bar shows what could inspire and justify the worries about the financial future. If you compute the same ratio, but for the numbers in the U.S. forecast in 2030, you can see that there will be fewer working-age adults, traditionally defined up to age 65, relative to each senior defined as age 65 and above. It is important to note that the U.S., unlike Japan and much of Europe (including Russia), will see growth in its labor force. This is because the number of working-age adults will decline when seen as a ratio compared to (divided by) the swelling numbers over age 64 forecast for the U.S.

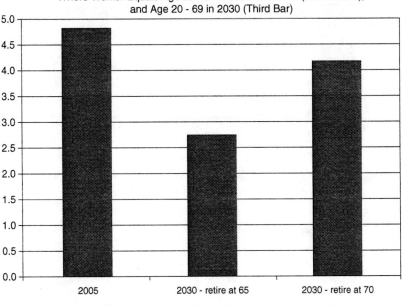

Worker to Retirees Ratio
Where Worker Equals Age 20 - 64 in 2005 and 2030 (Second Bar),
and Age 20 - 69 in 2030 (Third Bar)

Data source: U.S. Census Bureau International Database

If people still choose and are given incentives to retire at 65, you can see the reason for the pessimism. The key ratio portrayed in the preceding figure declines from nearly five to merely two and three-quarters, a huge decline. However, what if by 2030, people were given incentives, adult education and training, and the respect to motivate them to work until age 70? Of course, in reality, some will not or cannot work that long, but we believe this will be offset by many who would choose to work beyond 70. This book is replete with role models who work well beyond 70 and love it!

The third bar shows the ratio for the 2030 U.S. population forecasts again, except that it divides the number of adults ranging from age 20 to 69 by the age 70 and over. This change to a later average retirement increases the ratio two ways when compared to the "average retirement age of 65" that is currently shown for 2030 by the middle bar. One change is that there would be more workers for the U.S. workforce. These workers would be between ages 65 and 69, and they would add valuable experience to the workforce. The second change is that there would be fewer retired people. Combining these forces would radically reduce the need for financial pessimism because the key ratio would decline to only four and a quarter in 2030, which would be plenty of workers to fuel the economy and to ensure retirees were treated well.

Recall that this means gradually increasing the traditional retirement age, which would not reach age 70 until about 2030. Given current trends and forecasts, life expectancy will be significantly higher then, so people in 2030 and beyond who work to 70 can still expect long retirements on average. Impressively, U.S. life expectancy has been increasing about 1.5 years per decade. Physical limits will likely slow the increases, but almost all forecasts are for continued solid increases, with most predicting the U.S. average will exceed 80 by 2030, with women approaching 83. The U.S. Census Bureau, despite having relatively conservative estimates of increases in age longevity, predicts that the U.S. will have more than 12 million women 80 and older by 2030.

Even now, an average U.S. man who has had what it takes to reach 70 can look forward to 13.5 years of leisure even if he works until 70. A 70-year-old woman retiring now will average a retirement of over 16 years. In addition, a 70-year-old woman has a 33 percent chance of attaining age 90.

However, even in a future marked by long lives, some Americans may have adequate savings and will want to retire before 70. That's fine and it should always be a free choice. Arrangements should also be made for workers who are in physically demanding jobs and may be unable to work until age 70 to retire or to gain training for new careers. Such "muscle" jobs are by now a small and declining share of the economy.

We believe that most Americans will want to work until the age of 70, and may even want to work well past that age, to maintain a healthy and fulfilling life. This book has shown that staying productive can help you prosper physically, mentally, spiritually, and financially. Role models portrayed earlier should inspire you to see that your older years can be a chance to perform a second or even third act in your life!

■■ Recommended Sources

Books

Brim, Orville Gilbert, et. al. *How Healthy Are We? A National Study of Well-Being at Midlife*. Chicago, IL: University of Chicago Press, 2004.

Brown, Helen Gurley. *I'm Wild Again: Snippets from My Life and a Few Brazen Thoughts*. New York: St. Martin's Press, 2000.

Carter, Jimmy, and Rosalynn Carter. *Everything to Gain: Making the Most of the Rest of Your Life*. New York: Random House, 1987.

Cathy, Truett S. *Eat Mor Chikin: Inspire More People*. Looking Glass Books, 2002.

Cooper, Dr. Kenneth. *Regaining The Power Of Youth At Any Age: Startling New Evidence From The Doctor Who Brought Us Aerobics, Controlling Cholesterol and The Antioxidant Revolution*. Nelson Books, 1999.

Dychtwald, Ken, and Daniel J. Kadlec. *The Power Years: A User's Guide to the Rest of Your Life,* Wiley, 2005.

Fuqua, J.B. *Fuqua*. Longstreet Press, 2002.

Kahn, Robert, and John Rowe. *Successful Aging*. New York: Dell Publishing, 1998.

Kotlikoff, Laurence J., and Scott Burns. *The Coming Generational Storm: What You Need to Know about America's Economic Future*. The MIT Press, 2004.

Mondavi, Robert, and Paul Chutkow. *Harvests of Joy: How the Good Life Became Great Business*. Orlando, FL: Harcourt Brace & Company, 1998.

Peterson, Peter G. *Running On Empty: How The Democratic and Republican Parties Are Bankrupting Our Future and What Americans Can Do About It*. Farrar, Straus and Giroux, 2004.

Roizen, Michael F. *Real Age: Are You As Young As You Can Be?* New York: HarperCollins, 1999.

Siegel, Jeremy J. *Stocks for the Long Run: The Definitive Guide to Financial Market Returns and Long-Term Investment Strategies*. McGraw-Hill, 2002.

Weil, Andrew. *Healthy Aging: A Lifelong Guide to Your Physical and Spiritual Well-Being*. Knopf, 2005.

Willcox, Bradley, Craig Wilcox, and Makoto Suzuki. *The Okinawa Program: How the World's Longest-Lived People Achieve Everlasting Health—And How You Can Too*. New York: Three Rivers Press, 2002.

Young, Andrew. *A Way Out of No Way: The Spiritual Memoirs of Andrew Young*. Thomas Nelson Publishers, 1994.

Ziglar, Zig. *See You at the Top*. Pelican Publishing Company, 2000.

Web Sites

www.aarp.org—Nonprofit organization with over 35 million members targeting people over 50. Does advocacy work but members can also find jobs through the organization, sign up for insurance products, and receive advice on everything from health to careers. *AARP The Magazine* is the world's largest circulation magazine.

www.careerjournal.com—Sister Web site of *The Wall Street Journal* online, this site offers well-researched articles and tools, such as a salary calculator, to help you in your career search.

www.census.gov—The government porthole for any piece of demographic information you'd like about the U.S. A treasure trove of facts and statistics.

www.drweil.com—Great source of healthy eating and living information from renowned physician Dr. Andrew Weil.

www.finance.yahoo.com—Easily accessible financial news and research tools, plus glossaries to help you cut through the jargon.

www.webmd.com—Still a definitive resource for practical medical information.

INDEX